I

A
Profit and Loss Statement

McGraw Hill Professional – Finance Made Easy Series

Financial success is the *raison d'être* of any business, and financial health of any organization is reflected in its financial statements. But it has been observed that managerial professionals often have inadequate understanding of finance and little time to read treatises on it. Further, financial statements are regarded as too complex to understand and left to be 'deciphered' by financial experts. Hence, cultivating a culture of awareness and transparency of finance is a prime imperative.

Finance Made Easy Series has been designed to impart management executives with adequate knowledge to understand and appreciate financial statements and their implications for the fiscal solvency of their firms. This series seeks to demystify apparently complex financial statements, and help create a finance-savvy executive class, the key to fiscally sound and successful businesses. A lucid, creative and concise exposition of financial statements—their components, jargons and computational methods—with short stories and numerical examples makes for engaging reading for busy professionals.

Titles in the series:

- How to Read a Balance Sheet
- How to Read a Profit and Loss Statement
- How to Read a Cash Flow Statement
- How to Analyze Financial Statements

McGraw Hill Professional – Finance Made Easy Series

How to Read A Profit and Loss Statement

Second Edition

N. Ramachandran

Director of Kochi Business School, Kochi, Kerala

Ram Kumar Kakani

Professor, Lal Bahadur Shastri National Academy of Administration, Mussoorie, Uttarakhand

McGraw Hill Education (India) Private Limited
NEW DELHI

McGraw Hill Education Offices

New Delhi New York St Louis San Francisco Auckland Bogotá Caracas
Kuala Lumpur Lisbon London Madrid Mexico City Milan Montreal
San Juan Santiago Singapore Sydney Tokyo Toronto

McGraw Hill Education (India) Private Limited

Published by McGraw Hill Education (India) Private Limited,
P-24, Green Park Extension, New Delhi 110 016.

How to Read a Profit and Loss Statement, 2e

Print Edition:
ISBN (13): 978-9-33-921408-1
ISBN (10): 9-33-921408-0

Ebook Edition:
E-ISBN (13): 978-93-5134-300-4
E-ISBN (10): 93-5134-300-6

Vice President and Managing Director: *Ajay Shukla*
Publishing Manager—Professional: *Mitadru Basu*
Sr. Copy Editor: *Neha Sharma*
DGM—Sales and Business Development—Professional: *S Girish*
Asst. Product Manager—BGR: *Priyanka Goel*
General Manager—Production: *Rajender P Ghansela*
Manager—Production: *Reji Kumar*

Typeset at Script Makers, 19, A1-B, DDA Market, Paschim Vihar, New Delhi 110 063 and printed at ***.

Cover Printer: ***

Cover Design: Kapil Gupta

***

Preface

A company can be considered viable only when its fiscal health is sound continuously over a certain period. In all probabilities, a company that has been incurring more losses compared to its profits for over a duration of five years, cannot survive for long. Hence, it is important that even the employers of an entity, such as HR mangers should have a good grip of the financial statements for taking better future strategic stands. A very well-known example of financial decisions gone wrong is Lehman Brothers, which had announced a loss of US $3.9 billion in the year 2008 and went bankrupt the same year.

Even in the smallest business, the proprietor or manager will need to have an accurate and up-to-date information about how much has been bought and sold; how much money has been received for sales; how much has been paid away for purchases, etc. Private individuals often find it convenient to have the same information from their cash receipts and payments. You can imagine that with a very large business, chaos would quickly result without this information.

The series of books, *Finance Made Easy*, has been written to impart management executives with the knowledge that they would require in order to understand basic financial statements. The series is an attempt at breaking the myth that financial statements like income statement, cashflow statement and balance sheet are too complex to comprehend. This particular book deals with the income statement. The primary purpose of a business enterprise is to generate profits for its owners. The income statement conveys the profitability of the business. It is by looking at this statement, that we gauge the success of a business. It also provides us insights on the improvements that need to be made to further enhance a firm's profitability. Hence, it becomes necessary for all the stakeholders of a business to have some rudimentary knowledge about the statement and the impact it has on the business.

It is our sincere attempt into making this book your ideal guide in getting you to that point of making ultimate financial judgments. The readers will appreciate the simple language in which this book is written so as to get across all the unfamiliar financial jargons and present the concepts in a very easily comprehensible format. This book aims at answering questions such as:

- What is the meaning of a profit and loss statement?
- What goes into framing it and making it an important part of the financial statements?
- What is the basis of those items that are included in it?
- How can one analyze a business' future based on them?

Last, but not the least, we would like to mention that the views reflected in this book are impersonal and do not intend to affect the ethics of any institution.

Neelakantan Ramachandran
Ram Kumar Kakani

Acknowledgments

Our peers at ICAI, IIM, IIT, XLRI, LBSNAA, SPJIMR and other academic organizations have continuously inspired our thinking. Our research associates have immensely contributed to the manuscript development of this book. We are indebted to:

- Shri Kush Verma, M.A., M.Phil., IAS
- Prof. Sesha Iyer, Ph.D.
- Shri Jayant Singh, MA (History), IRTS
- Ms. Shaniya Khanam, B.Sc., MBA
- Ms. Tooshima Sarkar, B.A., M.A.
- Ms. Melody Jhang, D.H.M.

We are also thankful to Pooja, Sunita, Seema, and Surendar for their inspiration, support and feedback.

We would like to thank, Priyanka Goel, Sindhu Ullas, Smita Kulshreshth and other team members of McGraw Hill Professional. In particular, we thank Neha Sharma, whose skillful persuasion and editorial work helped clarify and steady our work enormously.

Finally, we are very grateful to our family members, including Ananya, Aruna, Chinku, Dhruva Govind, Kannan, Karuna, Kriti, Kunju, Lakhpat Rai Goel, Leena, Rathi and Vipra. Thank you all!

Comments from readers are most welcome (Email: ramkumarkakani@gmail.com).

Neelakantan Ramachandran

Ram Kumar Kakani

Contents

Introduction

Profits earned are also one of the chief indicators of the efficiency of a business concern. It is of utmost importance that each and every employee of a company understands the role that the *need for income* plays in shaping the decisions of a concern.

If you can read a nutrition label or a baseball box score, you can learn to read basic financial statements. If you can follow a recipe or apply for a loan, you can learn basic accounting. The basics are not difficult yet they are not rocket science. A person without or with little understanding of calculation and projection of income (returns) would have a tough time in contributing anything of value to strategic organizational decisions.

If you are an HR head/manager or a production manager who does not understand the financial underpinnings that drive organizational decisions, you will not be in a position to add the value required at the executive team level. In order to calculate the amount of profits (or loss) of a firm, a statement is prepared by the financial managers of an entity. This *Income Statement is* also known as *Profit and Loss Account (P&L Account).*

You must be wondering why an organization would have to prepare an income statement while it has already prepared a balance sheet of its business over a certain period. The reason is, in the capitalist system of society's economic organization, the entrepreneurs determine the course of production and pricing of the output. For example, think of a milk producers cost of production and cost of selling (say, Mother Dairy). In the performance of this function, they are unconditionally and totally subject to the sovereignty of the consumers. If they fail to produce in the cheapest and best possible way those commodities which the consumers are asking for most urgently, they suffer losses and are finally eliminated from their entrepreneurial position. Other businessmen, who know better how to serve the consumers, replace them in the market.

The primary motive of running a business enterprise; say, Google Inc. is its income/profit. Yes, owners of Google Inc. would be happier with a high-profit firm than a non-profit making firm. Hence, the profits are the compensation derived by an entrepreneur for the capital invested and risks incurred in running a firm (think of the reasons for the existence of Google and its benefits to its owners).

1
CHAPTER

The Income Statement — An Introduction

The numbers in a company's financials reflect real life business events. A firm's financial condition is easier to understand if one can visualize the underlying truth of these essentially quantitative indicators. For example, before one starts crunching numbers, he/she should have an understanding of what the company does; the amount of manufacture and sale of products and/or services, and the industry in which it operates for certain duration.

One should not just look at a company's balance sheet without looking at its income statement. A strong income statement combined with a weak balance sheet might indicate short-term success, but potential long-term problems. A strong balance sheet matched with a troubling income statement might show some stability, but weak sales or profits may also indicate poor management, products, pricing or expense controls.

When starting a business, a firm is required to abide by the law in presenting its financial performance over a given period. Any business entity needs to compulsorily prepare the two financial statements given below:

- Balance Sheet
- Income Statement

These perhaps, are the most important and relevant credentials for an enterprise to reflect its financial performance. While we have discussed the balance sheet in our earlier book titled *'How to read a Balance Sheet-Second Edition'*, we will be elaborating on the income statement and its relationship with the balance sheet in this book.

Due to the primacy of income and the role played by it in shaping the decisions of a firm, a detailed analysis is required to understand the components that influence it. The need for information in this regard is addressed by preparing a detailed statement summarizing the increase and decrease in income, caused by revenues and expenses during the accounting period. Yes, an *income statement* is a statement dedicated exclusively to summarizing this!

An income statement, also known as the *statement of financial performance*, uses a simple mechanism to come up with the final profit or loss figure at the end of an accounting period. All the revenues and expenses of a particular period are put together, categorized, and presented in an orderly fashion. The difference between these two components is either *profit*, in case revenues are more than expenses; or *loss*, in case expenses are more than revenues. Mentioned below is a very simple definition of the profit and loss statement.

What is a Profit and Loss Statement?

It is an orderly list of all the revenues and expenses at the end of the financial period.The difference between revenues and expenses gives an estimate of the profit or loss over the period, i.e., the net earnings of the business.This record provides the information that shows the ability of a company to generate profit by increasing revenue and reducing costs.

The Profit and Loss statement is also known as an *income and expense statement*. The following are the terms that we need to keep in mind while preparing the profit and loss statement:

Revenue

This is the total amount of money received or to be received by a company for goods or services it provided during a certain time period. So, for example, if a firm sells laptops worth ₹ 2,000,000 and also renders maintenance services to a firm for ₹ 500,000, then the total revenue of the company would be ₹ 2,500,000.

Expenses

Expenses are referred to as the costs incurred in producing revenue by a company. Continuing with the previous example, if the firm incurred ₹ 1,200,000 as the cost of manufacturing the laptops and paid ₹ 200,000 to the mechanic for repairing them, then the total costs incurred by the firm would be ₹ 1,400,000.

The subsequent sections of the book will deal with revenues and expenses in much more detail.

While surfing through this chapter, just as any other reader, our FME mascot Bholuram gets stuck in a particular portion and raises a question to Finnova. Hereon, they both share a few informative and important conversations as they did in *How to Read a Balance Sheet-Second Edition*. Let us take you through this ride:-

Here follows a very simple example for our readers to understand the basic concept of profit and loss-

Bholuram: Hey Finnova, you have used the word *expenses* above. What is the difference between *costs* and *expenses*?

Finnova: Good question, Bhola! Although, many a times the words are used synonymously (we'll also use the two interchangeably in some places), there is a subtle difference between the two terms. Costs refer to all the outlays of the company. The company may pay for items such as, purchasing raw materials, paying salary to staff, paying for electricity, etc. All these items will be referred to as costs of the company. Expenses on the other hand refer to that portion of costs which is incurred by the company in some revenue generating activity.

Let us illustrate with the help of an example:

Bhola, suppose you need to supply 100 pens to a company. For that you need plastic as raw material. Now, instead of buying plastic to manufacture 100 pens, you buy enough to manufacture 1,500 pens. You do this for future orders and also to ensure that you do not run out of plastic (raw material stock). Now, you used plastic for only 100 pens, while the rest is still kept in your godown as raw material inventory. In this case, the money spent on buying plastics for 100 pens can only be termed as expenses as only that part of your money was used towards a revenue generating activity i.e, selling of pens, while the money spent on the entire 1,500 pens is your cost. In future, however, when you decide to manufacture the remaining 1,400 pens, those costs will also become your expenses.

Bholuram: That is awesome Finnova! Let me think of a few costs in my firm that'll become expenses later. The cost incurred by you on the coffee and samosa that you gave me yesterday must have already become an expense.

Example 1: The Story of Bala

Once upon a time in Ramgarh, Bala, a popular dosawala who prepared and sold mouth watering dosas(aka *dosai*) outside a popular management school, was busy registering a large amount of sale as always. Then one day, Bala's luck struck and he got an appointment letter from a catering services provider in a big city which proposed to offer him a salary of ₹ 5,000 per month.

Being an illiterate was Bala's weakness. He had never been able to calculate the profits from his dosa business. With this new job order on his shoulders, he found it difficult to ascertain as to which of the options (his business or the new job) would give him a better return. He approached one of the management students in his area, Ms. Amrapalli, for help.

Ms. Amrapalli asked Bala the following two questions:-

- Bala, what would be the monthly sales of your dosa business (in other words, what is your revenue)?
- Besides that, what expenses do you incur in your business?

Bala wrote down a list on a sheet of paper and handed it over to Ms. Amrapalli, saying-

These are the total number of sales and expenses that happen in a month:-

Total number of sales in a month:

- 240 cheese dosas which I sell for ₹ 22 each
- 300 plain dosas which I sell for ₹ 11 each
- 280 masala dosas which I sell for ₹ 20 each

Total expense in a month:-

- Dosa paste: ₹ 4 for each piece of all dosa (includes all types)
- Oil: Re 1 for each piece of dosa (includes all types)
- Cheese: ₹ 5 for each piece of cheese dosa
- Masala: ₹ 7 for each piece of masala dosa
- Rent: ₹ 1,000 per month

Ms. Amrapalli quickly did some calculations to find out the total revenues for the *dosawala* and listed them on one side of a blank paper (see Table 1.1 below).

The paper looked somewhat like this:

Table 1.1 Total Monthly Revenues of Bala

Item (1)	Pieces (2)	Selling price per piece (₹) (3)	Total revenue (₹) (2) * (3)
Cheese dosa Plain dosa Masala dosa	240 300 280	₹ 22 ₹ 11 ₹ 20	₹ 5,280 ₹ 3,300 ₹ 5,600
Total	**820**		**₹ 14,180**

Then, on another piece of paper, Ms. Amrapalli listed all the expenses of Bala (see Table 1.2). They looked somewhat like this.

Table 1.2 Total Monthly Expenses of Bala

Item (1)	Pieces (2)	Cost price per piece (₹) (3)	Total cost (₹) (2) * (3)
Dosa paste Oil Cheese Masala Rent	820 820 240 280 –	₹ 4 ₹ 1 ₹ 5 ₹ 7 –	₹ 3,280 ₹ 820 ₹ 1,200 ₹ 1,960 ₹ 1,000
Total	**2,160**		**₹ 8,260**

Being a systematic management student, Ms. Amrapalli now listed all the revenues on the right side and the costs on the left side to get a better comparison of the revenues and expenses. Table 1.3 shows this statement.

Table 1.3 Total Revenues and Expenses of Bala

Expenses	Amount (₹)	Revenues	Amount (₹)
Dosa paste Oil Cheese Masala Rent **Profit** (Revenues less costs)	3,280 820 1,200 1,960 1,000 5,920	Cheese dosa Plain dosa Masala dosa	5,280 3,300 5,600
Total	**14,180**	**Total**	**14,180**

Now we see that the total revenues listed on the right side come to ₹ 14,180. At the same time, the total costs sum up to ₹ 8,260. The difference between both these items, i.e., the revenues and the costs is equal to ₹ 5,920 (₹ 14,180 – ₹ 8,260) is the profit for Bala, also known as *net income*. This figure is greater than ₹ 5,000 which was being offered by the catering company. Thus, Bala decided to stay in the campus and carry on with the existing business.

The last statement that we just saw was nothing but the income statement for Bala, the *dosawala*, whereby, we listed his total revenues and total costs to eventually come up with the profits earned by him (for one month).

Importance of Income Statement

Management and owners, while looking at their business during a period, are interested in getting answers to a few mundane questions such as:

- Was it a good year or a bad year for the business?
- What was the volume of operations?
- What was the margin available on sales ?
- How was each rupee from sales distributed among the different expense items and profit?

All these questions cannot be answered with a balance sheet. Answering the above questions would need an additional financial statement addressed exclusively to summarize the revenue and expenses of a particular period. This statement is what is referred to variously as the *Income Statement*, the *Income Summary*, the *Profit and Loss Account* or the *Profit and Loss Summary*. Though a profit and loss statement of a company can have a number of uses, the primary uses can be listed as under:

- It informs the stakeholders of the profits of the company for a particular period.
- It offers a comparison with the performance in the past and informs them of the company's progress.
- It helps them to predict the future profits of the company.
- It informs them of the profit margins maintained by the business.
- It tells them of the composition of the expenses of the company; and helps in identifying few cost cutting measures.
- It offers a comparison with other companies of the same industry.

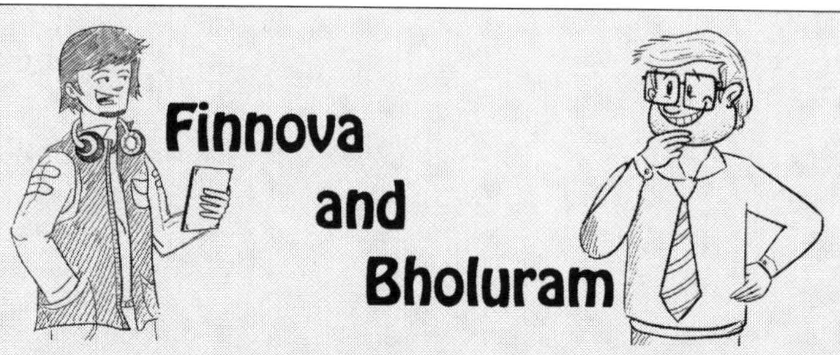

Bholuram: Hey Finnova, please tell me what is the difference between a Balance Sheet and Profit & Loss Account?

Finnova: See Bholu, the balance sheet is intended at reporting the value of the assets, liabilities and owners equity, at a particular point in time. It does not disclose any thing about the details of the operations of the business. It tells about the operation of the business during the period between previous year and present year balance sheet.

Both owners and the management are interested in knowing more about the changes in the owner(s) equity, in detail, and to address this information, a detailed statement summarizing the increase and decrease in the owner(s) equity, caused by revenue and expenses during the accounting period is prepared.

The primary motive of running a business enterprise is profits, so a detailed statement of the same is required to understand the components of the operations that influence profit and hence the need for the income statement.

Bholuram: Hmm..

Finnova: Bholu, are you thinking? That's something to watch for. Any plans growing in mind to set up your own business firm??

Bholuram: Nah, life is much easy now..I think I am better off without it.

2

CHAPTER

Accounting Principles

While preparing the accounts of a company, one comes across a number of alternatives with regards to accounting for certain items. Presence of such alternatives brings about a certain amount of ambiguity in the financial statements of a company. While dealing with the preparation of *income statement* too, there may be situations where more than one way of dealing with a component is possible. For example, if an order is received in one year (say, 2013), delivery for the good is made in the next year (say, 2014), and payment is received in the third year (say, 2015), then there may be confusion with respect to the year for which such revenue should be recorded.

In order to minimize such uncertainties, a number of principles or rules are framed which guide the accountant with respect to the steps to be taken – especially in presence of vagueness (as above). These principles form the basis on which the accounts of a company are prepared. These tell the accountant the specific ways in which a particular component should be dealt with.

Moving ahead, we first discuss what we mean by the term *accounting period*, following which, we list some of the most widely accepted principles with regards to the profit and loss account of a company.

Accounting Period

Accounting period is commonly referred as the *'financial year'* for which we make the financial statements of a business entity, i.e., a balance sheet and an income statement. The readers might have observed that most companies follow a time period either from *1st April to 31st March or* from *1st January to 31st December* as their accounting periods. But these accounting periods should not be considered as a compulsion by law (or accounting bodies). These are followed more as a matter of past convention and convenience.

Though rare, the business entities can have accounting periods of less than or more than 12 months. Legally, the maximum period may be of 15 months which may be extended to 18 months on obtaining special permission from the Registrar of Companies.

One can notice that in the example of Bala *dosawala*, in the previous chapter, the accounting period was of just one month for preparing Bala's income statement.

Realization Principle

Realization is technically understood as the process of converting a non-cash resource or a right into money. For example, selling of chairs for cash which has the effect of converting non-cash resource, i.e., chairs into money. In terms of accounting, it is more precisely understood to mean recognition of revenue from sale of assets for cash or other such receivables such as cheque, promissory notes, etc. Realization, pertains to the recognition of revenue from a sale or provision of goods or services to customers. *Realization principle* is used to precisely identify the amount of revenue to be recognized and the amount of expense to be matched to such revenue, for the purpose of income measurement.

"When should we recognize revenue?" This is the question that the realization principle tries to answer. There can be several arguments for and against recognizing revenue at a particular time, which could be the time when the inventory is acquired, when the goods are made ready for sale, when the order is received, when the goods are delivered, or when the sale proceeds are collected. In order to avoid such confusion, *revenue is generally recognized when goods are delivered or services are rendered.* This is done despite the fact that delivery is only one of a series of events related to the sale. The rationale is that delivery validates or in other words, confirms a claim against the customer. The customer is set to be obligated to the seller with regards to the payment for the goods (or services) received.

The principle of realization being the point of recognition of revenue also enables us to have a reference for recognizing the expenses incurred in making available such goods or services. Thus, the realization principle facilitates the process of income measurement by identifying revenues and expenses with respect to such revenues. By implication, if costs are incurred in producing the goods, unless sales are made, such costs are not considered as expenses. So, as soon as revenue is recognized, all the costs which went about realizing that revenue now form part of the expenses. These costs, which have become part of the expenses, are also known as *expired costs.*

To summarize the above discussion, the realization principle implies the following two major factors:

- All completed sales transactions of the period and the amounts received or to be received, with relation to such completed sales transactions are recognized as revenue of the period. Such sales transactions are generally taken to be complete only when the goods are actually delivered or service is rendered.
- All costs involved in the goods or services transferred to the customer are recognized as expired costs and are hence, expenses of the period.

Accrual Principle

Closely related to the realization principle is the accrual principle. Common sense dictates that measurement of an organization's income is the most important use of accounting. The managers need to be constantly updated with the income of their companies. The accurate measurement of income is enhanced via the use of the accrual principle of accountancy.

"What is income?" Well, it is essentially a measure of the change in owner(s) equity over a period of time. One example of a change in the owners' equity is that if you go to buy a shirt from a shop (say, ₹ 500), then the cash balance of the shop and the owner(s) equity will increase by an amount of ₹ 500. Similarly, if a company pays ₹ 1,000 cash towards purchase of a fan, then the cash balance of the company and its owner(s) equity will reduce by an amount of ₹ 1,000.

However, there will always be cases wherein, revenues and expenses would not be accompanied by a simultaneous increase/decrease in the cash position of the firm. It may happen that cash relating to the revenue of a particular period is realized in some other accounting period and cash relating to a particular expense item is paid out in a different accounting period. As in the previous example, the company might very well have paid the ₹ 1,000 it owed towards the purchase of the fan in the next accounting period. Recording of such non-cash transactions is one of the prime challenges in accounting. We use the accrual principle in order to deal with these discrepancies.

The accrual principle in turn takes the help of the most fundamental accounting equation:

★★★

Owner(s) Equity + Liabilities =
Assets Owner(s) Equity + Liabilities = Assets

★★★

According to this principle, the incoming and outgoing of cash is absolutely immaterial for calculating the income of a period. What the accountant should be concerned with is whether the transaction has any defect on the owners' equity and consequently on the equation. Only those transactions which have an effect on the owners' equity are taken into consideration when calculating the income of a specified period. Thus, by maintaining the accounts on an accrual system, a more accurate estimation of the income of an entity pertaining to that particular accounting period is observed.

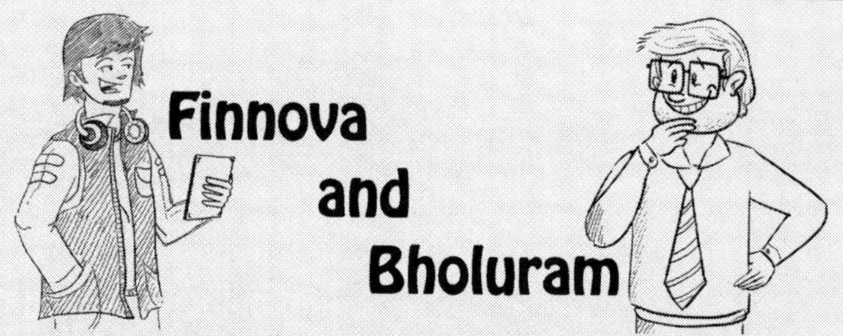

Bholuram: Hey, Finnova! What is Owners' Equity? And why have you suddenly raised your pitch?

Finnova: Bhola, now I am convinced that you suffer from short term memory loss. Don't you remember that in the book on Balance Sheet, we defined the owners' equity as:

Owners' Capital + Reserves & Surplus + the Retained Profits of the Business Entity

It essentially gives us the amount of money that the owners, i.e., shareholders own in a company. It is important to note that with an increase in profits, the Owners' Equity will increase, while it will decrease in case of a loss. Consult your book on Balance Sheet for further details.

Bholuram: Thank you. Now, I am confident that you suffer from high blood pressure.

To summarize, the accrual concept states that net income arises from events that change the owner(s) equity in a specified period and that these are not necessarily the same as the change in the cash position of the business. Thus, realization and accrual together, lay down the ground rule for the measurement of income.

To better illustrate how these two principles help in the measurement of income, let us take up another example.

Example 2: The Case of Magma Gupta

Situation 1:

Ms. Magma Gupta started her business on July 1. On the same day, she took a loan of ₹ 1,000,000 from a bank at the rate of 12 percent per annum for purchasing machinery. The machinery has a life of 10 years, with no scrap value. She also paid ₹ 600,000 as three months' rent, in advance. Now we are required to calculate her expenses for the month of *July*.

Explanation

Readers will agree that the bank borrowing does not represent revenue. The increase in the cash is offset by an increase in the liabilities,whereas, an interest of ₹ 10,000 (computed as monthly charge equals ₹ 1,000,000 × 12% × 1/12) and a depreciation of ₹ 8,330 (computed as monthly charge equals ₹ 1,000,000/10 × 1/12) are accrued expenses in the month of July. Rent expense for the month of July will be ₹ 200,000 only, as the rent has been paid in advance for the months of August and September.

Situation 2:

Magma had received written orders worth ₹ 2,000,000 in the month of June itself (even before starting her business). She started the production accordingly. The total cost of production was ₹ 1,200,000. The sales of merchandise to her customers, from 2nd July to 31st July 2013 are as follows:

Total Sales = ₹ 950,000 (cash sales = ₹ 250,000 and
Credit sales to Syed Shabbirul Haque = ₹ 700,000)

Explanation

In Situation 2, the revenue is recognized only when the goods are sold to the customers and not on receiving the order or on incurring the production cost. So, the total sales during the month of July would be ₹ 950,000. It is an amount equal to the cash received (₹ 250,000) and to be received in the later month (₹ 700,000). Thus, the accounting equation would be:

Assets = Liabilities + Owner(s) Equity

or

Cash + Debtors = Liabilities + Owner(s) Equity

Hence, ₹ 250,000 + ₹ 700,000 = ₹ 0 + ₹ 950,000.

When Syed Shabbirul Haque pays ₹ 700,000 in the next month, that amount must not be counted for the second time while measuring the revenue in the month of August. During that period (when cash is received from Syed Shabbirul Haque), the cash would increase by ₹ 700,000 and the debtors would decrease by the same amount. The amount of total assets, liabilities and owner(s) equity would remain the same.

The accrual concept plays an important role in the example discussed. Credit sales to Syed Shabbirul Haque are considered to be revenue earned in July, whereas the cash is received in the next month. Thus, the revenue is of July, when the sale took place, and not when the cash is received[1].

Table 2.1 presents the differences between the accrual and cash basis of accounting.

Table 2.1 ***Accrual System vs Cash System***

Basis of Accounting	Accrual Basis	Cash Basis
Revenue	When earned	When cash is collected
Expenses	When incurred	When cash is paid
GAAP Compliance	Yes	No

(Contd.)

[1]Herein, it would be worthwhile to mention that there are some business entities, which still prefer to maintain their accounts on cash rather than an accrual based system. They compute their income only on the basis of cash paid; and not when there is a change in owner(s) equity. Of course, most of these entities would have customers with poor payment records (resulting in doubtful receivables). Typically, small shops and village money-lenders are most prone to maintaining a cash-based accounting system.

Table 2.1 *(Contd.)*

Basis of Accounting	Accrual Basis	Cash Basis
Example	If you were a student staying in a hostel then your hostel owner would record an income event on the day your hostel rent comes due (you owe it to him/her). He/she records an expense event when he/she owes the monthly wages to the servant for maintenance of your apartment in that month (he/she owes it to the agent).	If you were a student staying in a hostel then your hostel owner would record an income event only when you pay your hostel rent. Similarly, the hostel owner records an expense event when he/she pays the wages for maintenance of the apartment.

Matching Principle

We agreed earlier that for business enterprises, it is absolutely essential to measure accurately the income of a particular accounting period.

This is where the matching principle comes handy. It states that while calculating the income for a particular accounting period, the costs for that period should be subtracted or matched with the revenues of that period. Then, we would be left with the profit or loss of the company for the period. It is this profit or loss that will get added or subtracted from the owner(s) equity. So, by matching the revenues and costs of the same period, a precise measure of the net income (or loss) of that particular period is made possible by the matching principle.

The examples of the use of matching principle include the following:

- **Deferred Taxation**

  It requires the accounting for taxable and deductible temporary differences arising in the calculation of income tax in a manner that results in the matching of tax expense with the accounting profit earned during a period. For example, purchase of a new vehicle results in payment of "road tax" for a period of fifteen years in advance. This will get periodically adjusted i.e., this periodic 'road tax' will be reflected as an *expense* item in the future years (as the vehicle's life changes).

- **Cost of Goods Sold**

  The cost incurred in the manufacture or procurement of inventory is charged to the income statement of the accounting period in which the inventory is sold. Therefore, any inventory remaining unsold at the end of an accounting period is excluded from the computation of cost of goods sold. We shall give you illustrations of this one in the next few chapters.

The understanding of the basic accounting principles helps us to understand and analyze an accounting period. Following are some of the most important ones in Table 2.2.[2]

Table 2.2 ***Basic Accounting Principles***

Basic Accounting Principles	What It Means in Relationship to a Financial Statement
1. Business Entity Assumption	For all legal purposes, a sole proprietorship and its owner are considered to be one entity, but for all the business transactions, they are kept distinct and separate from that of the owners' personal transactions by the accountant.
2. Monetary Unit Assumption	Owing to this principle, an accountant tends to ignore the fact that a currency's purchasing power changes over time with the effect of inflation on recorded amounts. For example, Rupees value from a year 2000 transaction is combined or shown with Rupees value from a year 2014 transaction.
3. Time Period Assumption	The period of time should be shown in the heading of each income statement. For example, the reader needs to know more than just the date "31st March", i.e. the statements for different time periods should be shown differently, as in - the *one week* ended 31 March, 2014 or the *month* ended 31 March, 2014 or the *three months* ended 31 March, 2014 or the *year ended* 31 March, 2014.
4. Cost Principle	The term "cost" is referred to as the amount spent on something purchased or obtained (either through cash or any cash equivalent). The amounts shown on the financial statements are referred to as *historical* cost amounts since these purchases may have happened during the current year, last year or long time back ago.[3]

(Contd.)

[2]Generally accepted accounting principles (GAAP) refer to the standard framework of guidelines for financial accounting used in any given jurisdiction; generally known as accounting standards or standard accounting practice. These include the standards, conventions, and rules that accountants follow in recording and summarizing and in the preparation of financial statements. Those principles have been brought forth to the readers via this chapter.

[3]Because of this accounting principle asset amounts are not adjusted upward for inflation. In fact, as a general rule, asset amounts are not adjusted to reflect any type of increase in value. Hence, an asset amount does not reflect the amount of money a company would receive if it were to sell the asset at today's market value. (An exception is certain capital market investments that are actively traded on a stock exchange).

Table 2.2 *(Contd.)*

Basic Accounting Principles	What It Means in Relationship to a Financial Statement
5. Full Disclosure Principle	Every information necessary for an investor analyzing a company's financial statements, should be conveyed through the statement itself or needs to be mentioned in the notes or footnotes below the statement. Every company lists its significant accounting policies as the first note to its financial statements. As an example, let's say "State Bank of India" stands as a bank guarantor for one of its clients for a small fee (to enable it to do further business). When State Bank of India's financial statements are being prepared it is always clear about the client's ability w.r.t bank guarantee instrument. As a result of this condition and because of the full disclosure principle, the 'Bank Guarantee' amount will be described in the notes to the financial statements. Most banks have large amounts of 'Bank Guarantees' mentioned as part of the footnote.
6. Going Concern Principle	The concept of going concern looks at business entities as having a life of an infinite duration. This accounting principle assumes that a company will not liquidate in the near future. If the company's financial situation does not look good, then the accountant needs to mention this assessment. A company can take advantage of this and postpone some of its prepaid expenses until future accounting periods.
7. Materiality	Materiality is the practice of not bothering about trivial values. According to this principle, an accountant might be allowed to violate another accounting principle if an item's amount is insignificant. For example, the purchase of a printer worth just ₹ 35,000 by a highly profitable multi-million dollar company hints that the printer will be used for five years.This guideline may violate the matching principle and allow ₹ 35,000 to be shown as expensed in the first year instead of ₹ 7,000 being expensed in each of the five years that it is used.

Assets that Become Expenses

Almost all the assets a business entity owns sooner or later become expenses, a concept called *asset expiration*. We also observe a few assets such as inventories becoming expenses sooner than later. An examination of some specific cases of assets that become expenses will enable us to understand the idea of asset expirations very clearly.

Inventories

Inventories[4] of merchandise become expenses when they are sold. A trader selling off his inventory is a simple example of inventories becoming expenses. In case of manufacturing organizations, all the costs incurred on the transformation of raw materials add value to the inventory. These costs are treated as expenses only when the inventory in question is sold (based on the realization and matching principles).

Prepaid Expenses

Prepaid expenses[5] represent services or assets paid for, prior to their actual use. Thus, they represent unexpired costs. They become expenses when the services are used or assets are consumed. Railway reservation tickets purchased a couple of weeks before the actual travel, by a firm, is a good example of a prepaid expense. When the travel dates on the ticket lapses, the prepaid expense gets converted to an expense. Prepaid rent and prepaid insurance are other examples of prepaid expenses.

Long-Lived Assets

Fixed assets such as furniture, plant and machinery, and vehicles have a limited useful life. The costs of such assets expire during the life of the assets in question. Such expiration of the costs of the assets is referred to as *depreciation* capturing the decreasing future utility of these assets. Chapter 6 is entirely devoted to explaining the concept of depreciation.

---

[4]Though this topic was introduced in the book *How to Read a Balance Sheet-Second Edition,* the coverage here is from the perspective of profit and loss statement.

[5]Refer to the book *How to Read a Balance Sheet-Second Edition* for better understanding of this book.

3

CHAPTER

Measurement of Income

When you sell an item costing ₹ 7,000 for ₹ 10,000, assuming no other costs, you earn a profit of ₹ 3,000. What we have done in arriving at this conclusion is nothing but a measurement of the net income. This is achieved by comparing the revenue from sales against the cost of materials parted with for earning that revenue. The net difference in this comparison represents *net income* or *profit*.

The simple illustration demonstrates the basic process of profit measurement. This process involves the following steps shown in Fig. 3.1.

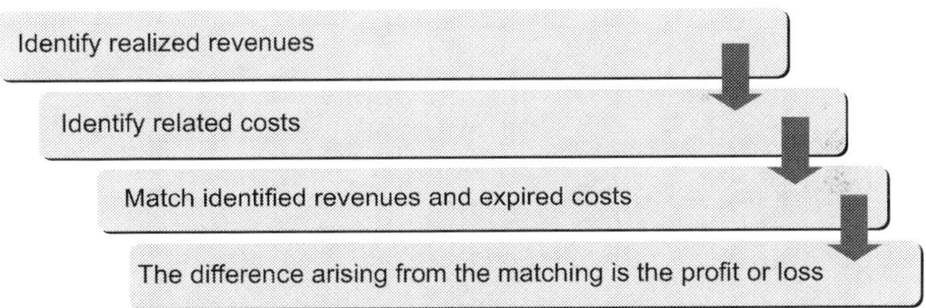

Figure 3.1 ***Measuring Profit or Net Income***

- First, identify the realized revenues.
- Second, identify the costs expiring in relation to those identified revenues.
- Finally, match the identified revenue and the expired costs. The difference arising from this matching is the *profit* (when revenue is higher) or *loss* (when costs are higher).

Revenue

Revenue may be understood as the total amount of money received or to be received by a company in return of goods sold or services provided to some other entity. It also includes earnings from interest, dividend, rents and other items of income. Furthermore, it is referred to as *sales* or *turnover*. It is to be noted that in the accrual system, revenue is a measure of the total sales/ revenue accrued or earned for the period, irrespective of whether or not any cash is received in lieu of those liabilities.[6] If the right to receive that income is created or the time for which the income relates has expired, we treat the income as accrued.

For example, a credit sale made during this period, to be collected during the next accounting period, is an income of this period. Similarly, expiry of date and time for a non-cancellable hotel booking is an income for the hotel. Likewise, will be the case in a non-cancellable airline ticket.

Somewhat contrary to the concept of accrued revenue is unearned revenue. It refers to revenues being pre-received by a company in a particular accounting period, while it actually pertains to a later accounting period.

For example, if on March 5, 2013, a computer vendor received ₹ 500,000 as fees for annual maintenance from an education institution (say, IIT Kanpur) for the period covering April 1, 2013 to March 31, 2014, then the entire income of ₹ 500,000 would be treated as an *advance from customer* also popularly known as *unearned revenue*. Quite logically, unearned revenue is not regarded as the revenue of the current period but added to the revenue of the period to which it relates. In the annual maintenance example, the amount of ₹ 500,000 will be regarded as revenue for the accounting period beginning on April 1, 2013 i.e., financial year 2014 and not financial year ending March 31, 2013.

Characteristics of Revenue

- Normally, revenue is generated out of business activities, i.e., sale of goods or rendering of services.
- Revenue results in an inflow of assets (cash or receivables) and an outflow of goods or services (cash or payables).
- Revenue is usually related to a specific period i.e. revenue of one year cannot be included as revenue of another year.
- Revenue leads to an increase in the owner(s) equity.

It is important to note that revenue should not be confused with *profit* or *net income*. Revenue arises throughout the accounting period by way of sale of goods

[6]Obviously, the time of "recognition of revenue" for companies following the accrual system of accounts will be different from companies following the cash system of maintaining accounts.

or rendering of services, but profit is to be calculated at the end of the accounting period. Profit is calculated by matching the revenues with the costs that have been expired during the relevant accounting period, wherein revenues *less* expenses gives us the profit for the period.

Expenses

Expenses are costs incurred and expired in connection with the earning of revenue. An expense is a sacrifice made or resource consumed in relation to the revenues earned during an accounting period. It is to be noted that cost and expenses do not mean the same thing. Only costs that have expired during an accounting period are treated as expense. Costs incurred do not become expenses until the goods (or service) in question are exchanged or the accounting period in question is over (please refer to the first conversation between Finnova and Bholuram on Page 4 to review the concept).

Expenses of a given period are:

- *Costs and expenses of the current accounting period* are costs incurred during the accounting period, which also expire during the same period. For example, cost of materials bought and sold during the same accounting period.
- *Costs incurred in a previous accounting period* that become expenses or expired costs during the current accounting period. For example, inventory purchased during the previous period, but unsold during that period and sold during this period. The amount of inventory, which represented unexpired costs and hence, an asset at the close of the previous accounting period becomes expired costs and is treated as an expense during the period in which it is sold.
- *Expenses of this year, the monetary outlay for which will be made during a subsequent period* are also expired costs of the current period, but the costs are incurred by contracting a liability. For example, rent which is due for the current accounting period, but is to be paid in the next accounting period.

As discussed earlier, *Owners' Equity plus Liabilities equal to Assets*

Any transaction that has the effect of reducing the assets or increasing the liabilities, results in a decrease in the owners' equity. Such a transaction is treated as expense. For example, rent paid for an amount say, ₹ 15,000 will have the effect of decreasing an asset (cash) and consequently, decreasing the owners' equity, hence, this ₹ 15,000 will be taken as expenses for the period.

Classification

All the costs (and expenses) incurred by a business can be grouped into two broad categories—inventoriable costs and non-inventoriable costs.

★★★

Inventoriable Costs *are all those costs that can be directly or indirectly, traced or tracked to the goods or services in question and can be regarded as expiring with the passing of title to the buyer.*

★★★

Non-inventoriable Costs *are all other costs incurred during a period, which would not leave behind any value with the passage of time. Examples of such costs could be rentals paid for offices, interest paid on borrowings and so on. These are recognized as expenses with the expiration of the specific accounting period.*

Non-inventoriable costs are usually period costs and hence are to be matched against the revenues of the period. Example 3 will help in clearing any confusion with regards to inventoriable and non-inventoriable costs.

Example 3: Maninder Singh

Maninder Singh purchased merchandise worth ₹ 100,000 during the fiscal year 2013-14. Being adept at business, he sold half the merchandise during the period for ₹ 75,000. He incurred ₹ 20,000 as warehouse rent for storage of the merchandise. Now, at the end of the year, it was time to give a report on the financial health of his business to his father. Confused with respect to the classification of a number of items, he called upon Christina Chongthu to help him. Being good at accountancy, Christina accurately classified the items on the following basis as depicted in Table 3.1.

Different Accounting Period Items

We can observe that there are two ways by which the cash paid and the expenses related to (the cash paid), occur in different accounting periods:

Table 3.1 ***Classification of Items***

Item	Remarks
Cost of inventory ₹ 100,000	The purchase prices of the merchandise.
Increase in owners' equity, i.e., Revenue ₹ 75,000	The sale proceeds realized in exchange of one half of the merchandise.
Expenses, i.e., expiration of inventoriable costs ₹ 50,000	The cost of the merchandise parted with or given over to the customer in exchange for the revenue. The reduction in owner(s) equity as a result of reduction of inventory. The cost with respect to the revenue earned and hence expired cost.
Expenses, i.e., expiration of non-inventoriable costs ₹ 20,000	The cost of rent for the facility is a cost incurred during the period and expiring during the period, i.e., a period cost. Note here, that the entire cost of ₹ 20,000 is taken as expenses and it is not apportioned between sold and unsold inventory.
Ending inventory ₹ 50,000	The unexpired cost and hence an asset. A merchandise inventory as a convention is valued at cost.

1. Cash is paid prior to the incurrence of expense. In this case, at the time of payment of cash, an asset, classified as *prepaid expense* is created, an example of which would be *prepaid rent.*
2. Cash is paid after the incurrence of expense. In this case, at the time the expense is incurred as a liability, classified as *accrued* or *outstanding liability* is created. Examples of this would be *outstanding salary* and *taxes payable.*

Characteristics of Expenses

- Expenses are incurred for the purpose of generating revenue or benefit.
- Benefit is usually derived during the same accounting period.
- It is related to a particular period. However, the payment can be made before the recognition of the expense or afterwards.
- An expense leads to decreases in the owner's equity.

As already mentioned, expenses of an accounting period are subtracted from the revenues of an accounting period to give income of the accounting period. Hence,

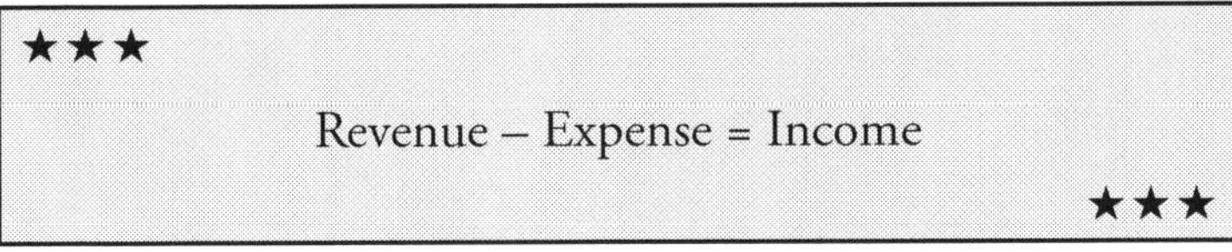

Before we go into the next chapter and come across more concepts, we present below the Profit & Loss Account of a listed company, *Reliance Industries Limited* (with a hope that this generates some more interest in the reader):

Table 3.2 **Profit and Loss Account of Reliance Industries Limited for the year Ended March 31, 2013**

Particulars	31-Mar-13 (Figures in Million)	31-Mar-12 (Figures in Million)
INCOME		
Revenue from operations/Net Sales	3,970,620	3,585,010
Other Income	78,670	61,940
Total Income (A)	**4,049,290**	**3,646,950**
Expenditure		
Cost of Goods Sold	3,322,500	2,981,910
Administrative & Selling Expenses	317,670	258,020
Financial Charges	34,630	28,930
Depreciation	112,320	124,010
Total Expenses (B)	**3,787,120**	**3,392,870**
Profit Before Exceptional Item and Tax (A-B)	**262,170**	**254,080**
Profit Before Tax		
Current Tax	53,270	52,260
DeferredTax	40	4,650
Minority Interest	70	70
Profit After Tax	**208,790**	**197,240**

Revenue from operations/Net Sales: Provides detail as to which products or services are major revenue items; it presents the sales, discounts, allowances and other related information to arrive at the net sales

Other Income: It indicates the income earned or gains resulting from non-operative transactions

Cost of Goods Sold: It is the cost to the company to generate the sales shown in Sales above.

Administrative & Selling Expenses: These are the costs associated with running the company as opposed to the costs of making or buying the products. It includes items such as salaries, rents, printing & stationery, legal expenses, consulting, agents' commission, advertising expenses, audit fees, etc.

Profit Before Tax: After subtracting finance charges and depreciation, an amount on which the company expects to pay taxes.

Current Tax: Tax to be paid within the given period in the same year.

DeferredTax: It is the tax that is payable in the future.

Minority Interest: It is a significant but non-controlling ownership of less than 50% of a company's voting shares by either an investor or another company.

Profit After Tax: This is the profit the company has earned for its equity investors (owners).

Bholuram: Finnova, I have a doubt regarding all the financial statements in general.

Finnova: Go ahead Bhola bhai – I am there to clarify them ☺

Bholuram: Just the way we have seen the Profit and Loss statement of ACC, how do I know if the audited financial statements in the annual reports of the other similar firms accurately reflect the financial position of a firm?

Finnova: The auditor's opinion is for advising the investors whether the financial statements of a firm provide an accurate financial picture. For this, the auditor must be qualified and should be a member in good standing of a professional accounting association recognized by the province. For example, the above financial statements of ACC Limited are audited by the auditors, "S.R. Batliboi & Co. LLP," Mumbai.

The other important requirements are:

- The firm's financial managers (especially, the CFO i.e., Chief Financial Officer) are responsible to have their accountants honestly prepare an interim (say, quarterly) financial statements, as well as, annual year-end financial statements.
- The firm must hire an independent and professional auditor to review the financial systems and records.
- The auditor's job is to determine the completeness and fairness of the financial statements, in all significant respects. Obviously, the auditors cannot review each and every financial transaction. The auditors perform such tests of the financial records, as they deem necessary in order for them to be able to provide a written professional opinion on the financial statements (for example, for a few randomly selected transactions, they verify the documents).

Is that good enough Bhola??

Bholuram: Yes, it suffices most of my doubts ☺

Preparation of Income Statement

An income statement is a summary of all the accounts dealing with transactions relating to revenue and expenses.

It is an account which shows the revenue generated from sale of goods and services and expenses incurred against such revenue, over an accounting period. It is also referred to as a *Profit and Loss Account.*

Account

An *account* is a statement, wherein information relating to an item or a group of similar items is accumulated. Such information is accumulated in a way that makes it very easy to display, summarize and analyze such information. An *income statement* is nothing but a summarization of all such individual accounts, relating to the elements of *expense* and *revenue. Let us explain this in some detail:*

To reiterate, the balance sheet equation was stated as:

★★★

Owner's Equity + Liability = Assets

★★★

Based on the first conversation between Finnova and Bholuram, the Owner's Equity in the above term can easily listed as:

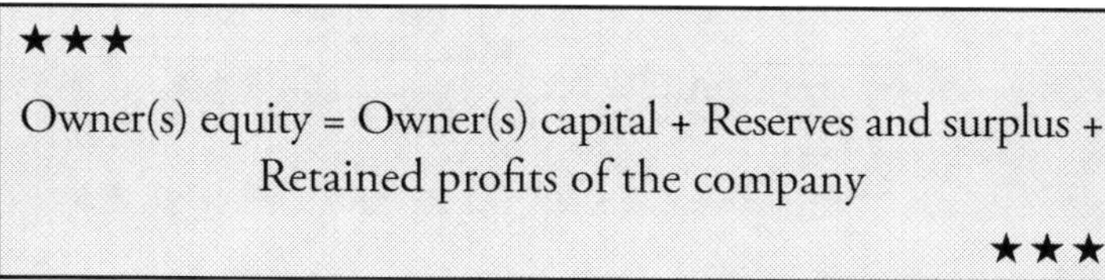

★★★

Owner(s) equity = Owner(s) capital + Reserves and surplus + Retained profits of the company

★★★

In the preceding equation, the *retained profit* of the company is nothing but the profit earned by the company less total dividends and drawings – wherein, *Total dividends* and *drawings* refer to that portion of the profits that is distributed to the owners of the business. The profit left is used to conduct business by the company and is also known as *profit reinvested* or *profit ploughed back* in the business. So, the *retained profits* can be written as:

★★★

Retained Profits = Profits – Total dividends and drawings

★★★

Now, since profits are nothing but revenue less expenses, the formula for *retained earnings* may also be expressed as:

★★★

$$RE = R - E - D$$

★★★

Here,

RE denotes Retained earnings
R denotes Revenue (or sales)
E denotes Expenses
D denotes Dividends and drawings

Readers, for a better understanding, let us now understand the discussed concepts with the help of an example.

Example 4: Ramsons

During an accounting period, Ramsons buys 12 units of inventory for ₹ 12,000. Another 10 units are purchased on credit, for ₹ 10,000. As many as 15 units of inventory were sold during the period, on credit, for ₹ 22,500. Five units of inventory were sold for cash, for ₹ 7,500, during the same period. We are required to prepare the profit and loss account of Ramsons for the given period.

To prepare the profit and loss account for the period, we would have to identify the realized revenues for the period and the corresponding expired costs or expenses (Table 4.1) to be matched against such revenue.

We have recognized ₹ 30,000 as realized revenue, irrespective of whether cash is collected or not. In other words, for the purposes of revenue recognition, both credit and cash sales are recognized as realized revenue. Now, the expenses of the period or expired costs will have to be reckoned with in relation to the realized revenues.

Table 4.1 **Realized Revenue**

Revenue of the period	Amount (₹)
15 units sold on credit 5 units sold for cash	22,500 7,500
Total	**30,000**

The total cost incurred during the period is ₹ 22,000, for 22 units of inventory. The costs incurred during the period are also reckoned without having reference to whether the costs are actually paid for in cash or not. The costs being incurred resulted in the acquisition of an asset, namely, inventory.

In order to determine the expense of the period, we have to take recourse to the realization of the revenue.

Q. What portion of the unexpired cost expires in the process of earning the revenue?
A. That expired portion of the asset is the expense of the period.

In our example, 20 units of inventory were parted with for earning the revenue. Thus, ₹ 20,000, the cost of 20 units of inventory, is the expired cost or expense for the period. Remember, that part of this inventory was purchased on credit. Therefore, it follows that the expense in accounting need not imply a decrease in cash, just as revenue need not imply an increase in it.

The two units of inventory, costing ₹ 20,000 remaining unsold are assets or the *unexpired cost* and have no relevance to the idea of measurement of profit.

For the summary, see Table 4.2.

Table 4.2 **Summary**

Revenue of the period	Amount (₹)
15 units sold on credit 5 units sold for cash	22,500 7,500
Total revenue of the period	**30,000**
Less: Cost of goods sold or expired cost of inventory Profit of the period	20,000 10,000

Table 4.3 **Ramsons Profit and Loss Account (For the accounting period)**

Expenses	Amount (₹)	Revenues	Amount (₹)
Cost of goods sold Profit for the period	20,000 10,000	Sales	30,000
Total	**30,000**	**Total**	**30,000**

Table 4.4 **Ramsons Balance Sheet at the End of First Period**

Assets	Amount (₹)	Liabilities	Amount (₹)
Current assets	7,500	*Owner(s) equity*	30,000
Cash	22,500	Contributed capital Profit	7,000
Receivables			
Inventory	7,000		
Total	**37,000**	**Total**	**37,000**

Revenue *minus* expense or profit of the period is ₹ 10,000. We can present the same formally in Table 4.3 shown above.

In the case of Ramsons, we dealt with only direct revenue and direct expense. Revenue arose from two sale transactions—one on credit and the other on cash. The expense was one simple direct item of expense—the *cost of sale* or the recognition of expiration of inventory cost. Before we proceed to study a more complex example and a detailed profit and loss account we must discuss some of the expenses or *cost expirations,* which cannot be traced as directly as in the case of *cost of goods sold* and are mostly of the nature of *indirect expenses.*

There are expenses that are to be incurred by a business, such as rent, interest, and advertising, which are fairly difficult to be traced to particular units of revenue for the purpose of matching. At the same time, it is obvious that the cost incurred on these items does not create any discernible benefits in a future period or create a value that can be exchanged. These costs are generally attributable to the revenue earning power of an accounting period and can be safely considered as *expired costs* in relation to the realized revenues of a period. These costs are sometimes referred to as *period costs* and matched against the revenue of the period without tracing a direct relation to the revenues. Based on this discussion, we present two important equations (see the two boxes given below).

Income statement equation

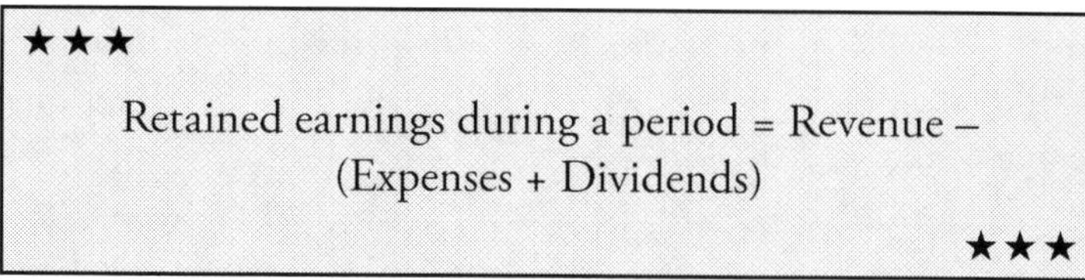

★★★

Retained earnings during a period = Revenue – (Expenses + Dividends)

★★★

Balance sheet equation

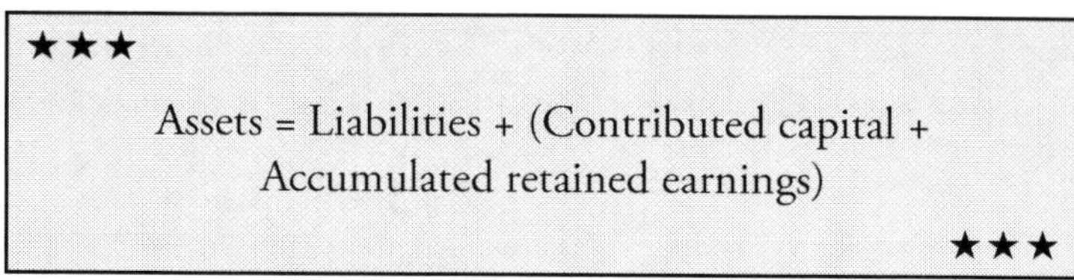

★★★

Assets = Liabilities + (Contributed capital + Accumulated retained earnings)

★★★

Readers can try to look at example 4 on page 27–29 using the two equations, to see if the balance sheet and income summary created go with each other. Before we get into a real life income statement, we will spend a little more time on understanding the various types of profits that we come across in the corporate language.

Various Types of Profit

The profit and loss account reflects the financial health of a company. There are various proportions of profit and loss which are addressed by separate expressions.

Gross Profit

The gross profit or gross margin is obtained by subtracting the cost of goods sold from the sales revenue. Direct costs in the production of goods or in the delivery of services are part of the cost of goods sold. Thus, in a manufacturing enterprise, the raw materials that go into making a finished product are part of cost of goods sold. A detailed discussion with respect to the cost of goods sold will follow later in the chapter.

Operating Profit

Operating profit is the figure obtained after subtracting operating expenses from gross profit. Operating expenses are those expenses which the business incurs in the normal course of operations like personnel, depreciation and other expenses.[7] Operating profit is the surplus generated by the normal operations of the company. The company, irrespective of the method of financing, earns this amount. This is a measure of the operational efficiency of the company.[8] We will discuss operating profit and operating expenses of a company in more detail, later in the chapter.

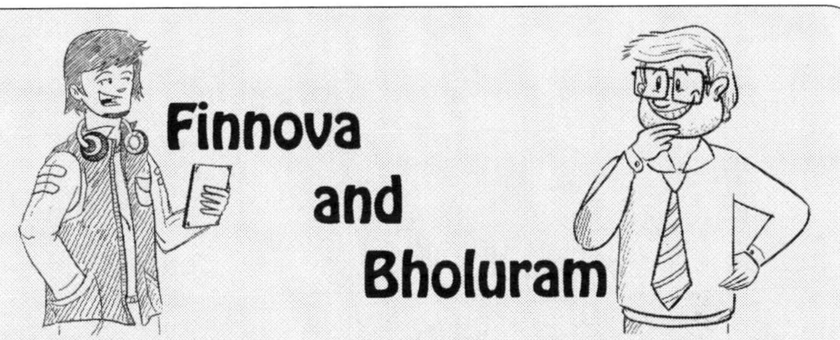

Bholuram: What do you mean by normal operations of the company?

Finnova: Look Bhola, a business or a firm is set up to perform a particular activity. It regularly performs that activity and derives profit by virtue of performing that activity. Such operations and such income, derived from the main-line of the business is known as operating income/operating profit. Apart from this core activity, a firm may also end up deriving profit from certain other non-core activities of the business. These activities fall outside the purview of the normal operations of the business and any income derived from these are known as non-operating income.

To give you an example, a wholesale vegetable vendor may derive some income, both from selling vegetables and from interest that it earns as a result of providing a credit facility to one of the customers. Here, income derived from selling of vegetables forms the core activity of the grocery store and is classified as operating income, while interest income earned is derived from an activity that does not form part of the core activity of the business and is incidental to it. Such income is hence, classified as non-operating income. We will list more examples of non-operating income, later in the chapter.

Bholuram: That reminds me that I have to purchase some vegetables for home. Otherwise, I will get a good thrashing from my life partner ☺ !!

[7]Expenses such as interest, finance charges/fees, and expenses incurred in the process of selling of a fixed asset, one-time registration costs, which do not form part of the operating expenses are known as *non-operating expenses.*

[8] Since it does not cover non-operating activities such as interest cost (of a loan) and sale/purchase of investments, hence non-operating incomes and expenses which are related to investment or sale of assets are excluded from this profit computation.

Profit Before Interest & Tax (PBIT)

It is the annual profit of the company before deducting any interest or tax from it. It is a good measure of the managerial performance of the company. It is obtained by subtracting non-operating expenses (except interest) from operating profit.

Profit Before Tax (PBT)

It is the annual profit of the company before deducting any tax from it. We can obtain this by simply deducting interest from PBIT. So, it clearly gives a fair view of activities and profit of the company without the burden of taxation.

Profit After Tax (PAT) or Net Profit

As the name indicates, it is obtained by deducting tax from PBT. It is the net income earned by a company after providing for tax and hence measures the net earnings to the owners of the company, i.e., its shareholders.

Profit Available for Distribution

This is obtained by summing up PAT and the retained earnings from previous years, i.e., the surplus balance of Profit or Loss Account raking from previous years. This is named so, as this figure gives us the total amount that the company can distribute to the shareholders of the company as *dividends* or *withdrawals*. This quite obviously includes the current year and the past year surpluses/profits (to the extent that have not been already distributed).

Appropriations

This is the last disclosure in the income statement and is figured out at its very bottom. It gives us the way in which the annual profit available for distribution is actually disposed of by the company. Appropriation includes items such as:

(i) **Transfer to reserves:** The part of the profits that the company retains in the business.

(ii) **Dividend to be paid to the shareholders:** The part of the profits that are distributed to the share holders as dividends.

Retained Earnings

It is normally derived by deducting the dividend to be paid to shareholders from the *profit available for distribution*. The discussed profit types may be easily represented in Flow chart 4.1 shown on next page.

Below is a live example of the Income Statement of Infosys Limited for the recent year.

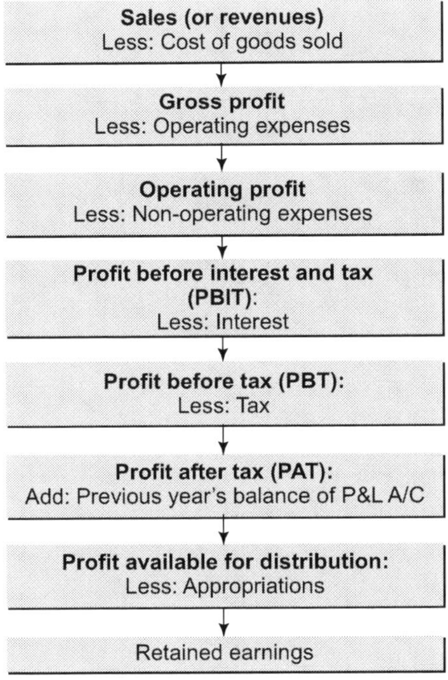

Flow Chart 4.1 ***Contents of Profit and Loss Account***

Form and Contents of Profit and Loss Account

So far, we have discussed the profit and loss account in the *accounts* format. It is also a common practice to present the revenue and expense information in a summarized *statement form* and to provide the details in attached schedules.

The method of presentation does not alter the results in any case, since the relationship is always:

★★★

Revenue – Expense = Profit (or Loss)

★★★

Example 1 **Profit & Loss Statement of Infosys Limited FY 2012-13 (all figures in ₹ millions)**

Financial Year ⇒	2013	2012
Sales / Income From Operations (A)	**403,520**	**337,340**
Less: Cost of Goods Sold (B)	263,100	208,930
Gross Profit (C→A-B)	140,420	128,410
Less: Sales, General & Administration Expenses(D)	24,240	21,180
EBIDTA[3] (Earnings Before Interest, Depreciation, Taxes & Amortization)(E→C-D)	**116,180**	**107,230**
Less: Depreciation & Amortization Expenses (F)	10,990	9,280
Operating Profit (G→E-F)	105,190	97,950
Adjusted for Other Income & Similar Items (H)	23,650	19,040
Adjusted for Exceptional Items (I)	(850)	-
EBIT (Earnings Before Interest Tax) (J→G+H+I)	127,990	116,990
Less: Interest Expenses & Financial Charges (K)	-	-
EBT (Earnings Before Tax, also known as, Profit Before Tax i.e., PBT) (L→J-K)	**127,990**	**116,990**
Less: Corporate Income Tax Expenses (M)	33,700	33,670
Net Profit (also, Profit After Tax i.e., PAT) (N→L-M)	**94,290**	**83,320**
No. of Shares (from Balance Sheet) (N)	570	570
Earnings Per Share (EPS) (O)	1,650	1,458

In the next page, there is a summarized income statement of one imaginary company, Arati Tools Limited in both the formats (see, Tables 4.5 and 4.6). We shall discuss the items presented subsequently. Most of the subsequent discussions would be based on this company's income statement.

[9]EBITDA is sometimes named OIBDA (operating income before depreciation and amortization). As the name suggests, this is earnings excluding expenses from depreciation, amortization, interest, and taxes (earnings + ITDA), in the order they usually appear on the income statement, up to down. *EBITDA Margin* is another measurement of a company's operating profitability. It is equal to EBITDA/ Total Revenue. EBITDA excludes depreciation and amortization; hence, nowadays most investors prefer EBITDA Margin as it gives a cleaner view of a company's core profitability.

Table 4.5 ***Accounts Format***

Profit and Loss Account of Arati Tools Limited for the Year Ended December 31, 2013 (all figures in ₹ millions)

Debit			Credit		
	Schedule	**Amount**		**Schedule**	**Amount**
Cost of goods sold	3	130	Sales net	1	255
Gross profit		130 260	Other income	2	5 260
Personnel expenses	4	49	Gross profit		130
Depreciation	5	11			
Other expenses	6	28			
Operating profit		42			
		130			130
Interest	7	12			
Profit before taxes		30	Operating income		42
		42			42
Income tax provision		12	Profit before taxes		30
Net profit after tax		18			
		30			30

Alternately, the same profit and loss account can be presented as follows:

Table 4.6 ***Statement Format***

Profit and Loss Account of Arati Tools Ltd. for the Year Ended December 31, 2013 (all figures in ₹ millions)

	Schedule	**Amount**
Sales net	1	255
Other income	2	5
Total revenue		**260**
Cost of goods sold	3	130
Gross profit		**130**
Operating expenses		
Personnel	4	49
Depreciation	5	11
Other expenses	6	28

(Contd.)

Table 4.6 **(Contd.)**

	Schedule	Amount
Operating profit		**42**
Interest	7	12
Profit before taxes		**30**
Income tax provision		12
Net profit after tax		**18**

The summarized profit and loss account will be accompanied by schedules, providing details for various items forming the total. For example, Schedule 7 (see, table 4.13), which corresponds to interest, will contain details with respect to the different loans against which the interest is paid, the rate of interest applicable, the bank to which the interest is paid, etc.

Sales

The net sales amount shown in the profit and loss account is after deductions (worth ₹ 5 million) from gross sales. Schedule 1 (see, table 4.7) provides the detailed break-up of the sales, by different divisions of the company, as also

Table 4.7 **Break-up of Sales**

Schedule 1: Sales		**₹ (millions)**
Gross sales		260.00
Less: Sales returns and allowances	1.75	
Sales discount	3.25	5.00
Net sales		**255.00**
Domestic:		
Machine Tools group	83	
Watch group	87	
Tractor group	60	
Lamp group	13	
Dairy Machinery group	2	
Total domestic sales		**245.00**
Export:		
Machine Tools Group	6	
Watch Group	2	
Others	2	
Total export sales		**10.00**

by domestic market and export sales. We observe that Arati Tools Limited earns its maximum revenue from its machine tools and watch divisions.

Sales Returns and Allowance

Sales records are prepared as and when goods are shipped to customers. The customers may return goods that are not according to the specifications; are damaged or defective in such cases, a refund of the sale is made. If the transaction was a credit sale, the account receivable in question will be cancelled. It is also a usual practice for the customer to retain the goods and an allowance may be made to compensate the customer for the damage, change in specification, or any other deviation from the order.

Such refunds or allowances are separately accumulated and accounted for, for the purpose of monitoring and control by the management. As shown in Schedule 1(Table 4.7) of Arati Tools Limited, at the time of preparation of the profit and loss account, such allowances are set off against the gross sales and the net sales are taken as the operating revenue earned. Many companies may not disclose this information in published accounts as competitors may use it to their advantage.

Sales or Cash Discount

Sales discounts are reductions from the invoice price (gross sales price without accommodating cash discounts), granted for prompt payment of the invoice, within a specified time limit. These reductions are sometimes called *cash discounts.* In our illustration, Arati Tools Limited allowed ₹ 3.25 million as discounts to customers.

It is a usual practice to state the discount offered to a customer on the invoice. The terms of payment with regards to the amount of discount, conditions for discount, etc., are usually presented in short forms or symbols.

Examples of such short forms are:

- 'Net amount' or' No cash discount'–(N);
- 'Net Amount due at the end of the Month'–(N/EOM);
- Net a mount due in 30 days of invoice, no cash discounts–(N/30);
- A 3 percent discount if payment is made in 10 days, otherwise net amount to be paid in 30 days – (3/10, n/30).

We will just explain the last item – 3/10, n/30; in some greater detail. An invoice of 3/10, n/30 states that a three percent discount is offered if payment is made within 10 days. It also implies that if payment is not made within 10 days, the normal credit of 30 days can be availed. Suppose you have an invoice of ₹ 1,000 with '3/10, n/30', you are losing three percent for 20 days' credit. Converting this 3 percent for 20 days interest to annual terms, would cost you 360/20 x 3% = 60% per annum in equivalent interest! This knowledge will definitely help you in planning your short-term Finances more defectively.

A company can have different terms of payment for different type of customers. Usually, terms of payment depend on factors such as past track record and credit reputation of the customer. A big customer with a good track record will obviously be given better credit terms than a small one with an uncertain track record.

Bholuram: Hey Finnova! Will a company offer both Cash Discount and Trade Discount?

Finnova: Bhola, now I can see a glimpse of brain in you☺. Yes, companies can and do offer both cash discounts and sales discounts simultaneously. Larger a company is and larger the size of the order, more attractive (large) will be the cash discount and trade discount. While cash discount offered will be visible in the invoice but the trade discount offered will not be visible in the invoice note.

Bholuram: Got it! In such a case, the next time we do business with each other, I would prefer a trade discount from you and hefty one there. I would also eagerly look forward to some sales allowances from you☺.

Trade Discount

You will not find a mention of trade discount in the profit and loss accounts. It is a usual practice to make the adjustment for trade discount while calculating the invoice price itself. So, if sales price is ₹ 100 and a trade discount of 10 percent is allowed, the invoice price mentioned would be for ₹ 90 (being equal to ₹ 100 minus ₹ 10 by way of trade discount). Trade discounts are in general used when a manufacturer makes bulk sales to a wholesaler, or a wholesaler makes large sales to a retailer.

Non-Operating Income/Other Income

The revenue earned by an enterprise is usually bifurcated into two parts, operating income and non-operating income. As mentioned earlier (in the first Box in this chapter), *operating income* usually refers to the income derived from the main-line operations of the business. Other income usually arises from activities incidental to the business. Schedule 2 (Table 4.8) lists the details of income from non-operating receipts by Arati Tools Limited.

Table 4.8 ***Income from Non-operating Receipts***

Schedule 2: Other income	**₹ (millions)**
Interest – banks	0.50
Interest – staff and offices	1.20
Export incentives	1.80
Sales agency commission	0.50
Profit on sales of assets	0.30
Dividend on trade investments	0.20
Other miscellaneous income	0.50
Total	**5.00**

Cost of Goods Sold

The computation of the cost of goods sold is very complex in the case of a multi-product, multi-division company, where you have large quantities of semi finished goods. In fact, the whole discipline of *costing* is primarily concerned with calculating the cost of goods sold. However, in simple cases where a trader deals in commodities and where each unit bought can be identified, costing becomes much easier affair. In order to calculate the cost of goods sold, we start the computation with the inventory that we have carried forward from the previous period and add all the expenses pertaining to the manufacturing part of the specified good. For example, in Schedule 3 (Table 4.9), we start with the inventory as on January 1, 2013.

Further, we add all the costs associated with the manufacturing of the goods in the year, i.e., purchase of material (purchase, other direct material costs), costs of material transportation (freight inwards) and cost of manufacturing (power, fuel). This provides us with the total goods that we have at our disposal for potential sale. Then we subtract the raw material and work in progress inventory at the end of the accounting period. This provides us with the total finished goods that we have at our disposal for potential sale. From this figure, we annually deduct the finished goods that is not sold during the period (i.e., retained and is classified as finished goods inventory) to get the cost of goods sold in this financial year. The cost of the goods sold in summary, presented in our illustration of Arati Tools Limited, can be understood more clearly from Schedule 3 (Table 4.9).

Table 4.9 ***Cost of Goods Sold***

Schedule 3: Cost of goods sold	**₹ (millions)**
Inventory on January 1, 2013	81.00
Add: Purchase	110.00
Freight-in	10.00
Other direct material costs	10.00
Fuel	3.00
Power	2.00
Total goods available	216.00
Less: Raw material and semi finished inventory on December 31, 2013	71.00
Goods available for sale	145.00
Less: Finished goods inventory on December 31, 2013	15.00
Cost of goods sold	**130.00**

Gross Profit

Gross profit or gross margin obtained by subtracting the cost of goods sold from the sales revenue, has great significance for a company. The cost of goods sold usually reflects the direct input costs and to a great extent, is variable with the volume of operations. In other words, cost of goods sold per unit of sales, is a fixed ratio. The gross profit, which is left after deduction of cost of goods sold, should be sufficient to cover all other operating expenses of the business. Only then will the business be viable and expected to turn a profit. Certainly, companies by and large try to maximize their gross profits by maximizing their total sales using the best combination of sales price and volume of business. Given a Fixed sales price, management and control of the gross margin will depend on improving the cost deficiency of operations and procurement.

Operating Expenses[10]

The cost of goods sold normally includes all costs of making the inventory available for sale, and are directly or indirectly traceable to the inventory to be sold. Examples of such costs would be cost of raw materials and cost of labor that went into making the goods. Apart from such costs, a firm also incurs some expenses towards running of its day to day affairs and managing the enterprise as a whole, like salary paid to the office staff, cost of stationery and rent paid for once. All those expenses, which are necessary to run the business enterprise or the organization, which are not directly associated with the company's output on a cause and defect relationship, are usually termed as *operating expenses*. It is possible to accumulate these expenses on the basis of material, personnel and other expenses, as in the case of the profit and loss account of Arati Tools Limited.

Personnel Expenses

Personnel expenses include remuneration and other benefits to the Staff and workmen. Schedule 4 (Table 4.10) details the expenses on account of personnel for Arati Tools Limited.

Table 4.10 ***Personnel Expenses***

Schedule 4: Personnel expenses	**₹ (millions)**
Salaries, wages and bonus	37.81
House rent allowance	2.19
Gratuity	0.75
Contribution to provident fund	2.75
Contribution to employees state insurance (ESI)	0.50
Workmen and staff welfare expense	5.00
Total	**49.00**

[10]Opex (Operating Expenses or Expenditure) is cost of goods sold plus general and administrative costs plus research and development costs which is the amount spent to keep a business running. It is used while making the income statement. Capex (Capital Expenses or Expenditure) is an investment in the business that adds value, such as the equipments required for a business. This equipment is then depreciated over an amount of time and the value eventually disappears. It is used while making the balance sheet.

For example, for an IT firm buying a computer is its CAPEX, and the annual cost of electricity and internet consumed is the OPEX.

Depreciation Expense

Depreciation is the expiration of costs of fixed assets. It is a usual practice to classify the depreciation expense according to the different groups of assets. In case of Arati Tools Limited, Schedule 5 (Table 4.11) gives the break-up of depreciation for the different groups of assets. We will discuss depreciation in more detail in a separate chapter.

Table 4.11 ***Depreciation***

Schedule 5: Depreciation	₹ (millions)
Fixed assets	9.84
Tools and Instruments	0.02
Patterns, jigs and fixtures	1.14
Total	**11.00**

Other Expenses

All the expenses other than those disclosed separately, are usually grouped together as *other expenses*. These expenses are relatively very small when considered as individual items. It is still customary to give a detailed break-up of the major items of operating expenses other than personnel, depreciation and financing costs. In case of Arati Tools Limited, the details are provided in Schedule 6 (Table 4.12).

Table 4.12 ***Other Expenses***

Schedule 6: Other Expenses	₹ (millions)
Power and fuel	3.10
Rent	0.50
Rates and taxes	0.40
Insurance	0.50
Water and electricity	0.60
Repairs to buildings	0.20
Repairs to machinery	0.80
Printing and stationery	0.90
Advertisement and publicity	2.40
Training	0.10
Audit fees	0.05
Royalties	0.85
Sole selling and other agents commission	4.70
Director(s)' fees	2.00

(*Contd.*)

Table 4.12 ***(Contd.)***

Schedule 6: Other Expenses	₹ (millions)
Provision for bad debts and advances	0.20
Loss on assets sold or discarded	1.30
Provision for warranty repairs	1.00
Miscellaneous expenses	8.40
Total	**28.00**

Operating Profit

Operating profit is the figure obtained after subtracting personnel, depreciation and other expenses, from the gross profit. The only other major expense to be met at this stage is the interest expense. Thus, operating profit is the surplus generated by the operations of the company. The company, irrespective of the method of financing (as interest is not accounted for), earns this amount. This is a measure of the operational efficiency of the company. This is also referred to as Earnings before Interest and Taxes (EBIT).

Interest Expense

The management has the option to Finance the assets from exclusively owner(s)' equity or with a combination of owner(s)' equity and borrowed funds (usually, through long-term liabilities). The interest part comes in if the management decides to use borrowed funds to finance either part or whole of the entity's assets from borrowed funds. In that case, interest is the compensation paid by the company to the lenders for parting with their money for a specified time. In the corporate world, most of the business entities use some amount of borrowed funds to finance themselves. Schedule 7 (Table 4.13) shows the different items of interest commitments of Arati Tools Limited.

Table 4.13 ***Items of Interest***

Schedule 7: Interest	₹ (millions)
Debentures	0.58
Fixed deposits	1.50
Loans from Government	5.00
Term loans from banks/financial institutions	0.42
Cash (packaging) credit from banks	3.50
Others	1.00
Total	**12.00**

Net Profit before Tax

Net profit before tax is the surplus after meeting all expenses, including interest. This is the profit available to the company as a result of both its operating as well as financing performance.

Income Tax

The profit before tax determines the level of taxation. As per tax laws, the amount of tax payable is not determined on the basis of the reported net profit. In most cases, some re-classification and adjustments have to be made to the profits arrived at by the firm to compute the taxable profit. These adjustments have to be made to accommodate the various income tax laws, provisions of which usually defer from the general accounting practices followed by the Firm.

To give you an example, tax laws in most countries, provide for tax concessions for investment in fixed assets, research and development, and so on. These allowances reduce the amount of tax payable by the company during the year in which such benefit is availed. Again, in most countries, tax concessions are also applicable to companies which earn income by way of exports in select sectors and for setting up investments/ infrastructure in backward and underdeveloped regions.

Net Profit or Profit after Tax

Profit after tax is the net amount of surplus earned by the company during the accounting period. This is the amount ultimately available to the company for appropriation, i.e., this amount can be either distributed as dividends to shareholders (owners) or retained in the business as retained earnings. Not distributing the profit among the owners increases the owner(s) investment, i.e., owner(s) equity in the business. From the shareholders perspective, the *profit after tax* (PAT) or *earnings after tax* (EAT) is the most important performance indicator of the company.

From the Corporate World

The Reliance Group, founded by Dhirubhai H. Ambani (1932-2002), is India's largest private sector enterprise, with businesses in the energy and materials value chain. *Reliance Industries Limited* is ranked 99th on Fortune Global 500 list of the world's biggest corporations for the year 2012.

Example 2 ***Income Statement—Reliance Industries Limited***

Profit and Loss Account for the Financial Years 2011 to 2013 Ended December 31 (all figures in ₹ millions)

Income	**FY2013**	**FY2012**	**FY2011**
Revenue from Operations	39,70,620	35,85,010	26,58,110
Other Income	78,670	61,940	25,430
Gross revenue	**40,49,290**	**36,46,950**	**26,83,540**
Expenditure			
Manufacturing expenses	33,22,500	29,81,910	20,44,240
Gross profit	726,790	665,040	639,300
Employee benefits expense	51,790	39,550	33,240
Finance costs	34,630	28,930	24,110
Depreciation & Amortization Expenses	112,320	124,010	141,210
Other expenses	265,880	218,470	200,190
Operating income (or operating profit)	**262,170**	**254,080**	**240,550**
Minority Interest	-70	70	220
Profit before tax	262,100	254,150	240,770
Current Tax	53,270	52,260	44,120
Deferred Tax	40	4,650	3,710
Profit after tax (or net income)	**208,790**	**197,240**	**192,940**

Income Statement and the Balance Sheet

Even when a company "owns" any other business entity, the two enterprises frequently remain separate legal entities with each responsible for its own bookkeeping. Stand alone Financial Statement refers to a statement of a single company or factory or unit or period, whereas consolidated financial statement refers to a statement prepared upon consolidation of two or more financial statements.

The importance of *profit* and its *measurement* in accounting, accords an important position to the income statement. However, it will be interesting to see how this financial statement is related to the balance sheet. Figure 5.1 captures the same.

Table 5.1 ***Relation of Financial Statement with Balance Sheet***

t_0	Accounting period - 1	t_1	Accounting period - 2	t_2
Balance Sheet (t0)	Profit & Loss Account for the first accounting period	Balance Sheet (t1)	Profit & Loss Account for the second accounting period	Balance Sheet (t2)

In other words, both of them are links in the information chain which make up the life of the enterprise.

While, balance sheet is a position statement at a point in time, income statement on the other hand summarizes an enterprise's performance over a period of time.

The ensuing discussion links both the financial statements of a business entity.

Please recall the basic balance sheet equation we have learnt in the previous lesson. We will repeat it for your convenience.

Assets = Liabilities + Owners' Equity **...(1)**

Here we need to keep in mind, that the owner(s)' capital need not be equal to the contributed capital, i.e., the amount of capital contributed to the capital by the owners; and is normally not the case. In fact, the owner(s)' equity changes with every sales transaction. How does this happen? The following two changes take part with every sales transaction:

- The amount of sales revenue realized increases owner(s) equity.
- The cost of goods parted with decreases owner(s) equity.

Therefore, the resultant increase in the owner(s) equity was equal to the net increase in the assets (sales revenue – cost of goods) i.e., equal to the *profit.* We explained an alternative representation of owner(s) equity in the previous lesson as being equivalent to:

Owners' Equity = Contributed Capital + Retained Earnings ...(2)

Combining equations (1) and (2) results in the expanded balance sheet equation as shown below:

Assets = Liabilities + Contributed Capital + Retained Earnings ...(3)

Based on the discussion in the previous chapters, we could write the income statement relationship as follows:

Retained earnings = Revenue – Expenses – Dividends ...(4)

Now, by just putting this representation of retained earnings in equation (4) in the balance sheet equation (3), we will get the following equation for assets:

Assets = Liabilities + Contributed Capital + Past Retained Earnings + Revenue – Expenses – Dividends ...(5)

The last three terms in equation (5) are referred to as the *profit and loss account* or *income summary.* But, the fact remains that the profit and loss account is an integral part of any balance sheet, where it is an expansion of one of the terms of the balance sheet. We reiterate our point with the help of Figure 5.1.

In other words, equation (5) can be restated as follows:

Assets = Liabilities + Contributed Capital + Beginning Retained Earnings Balance + Revenue – Expenses – Dividends ...(6)

The resulting new balance sheet of the enterprise can also be presented as follows:

Assets = Liabilities + Contributed Capital + Ending Balance Retained Earnings ...(7)

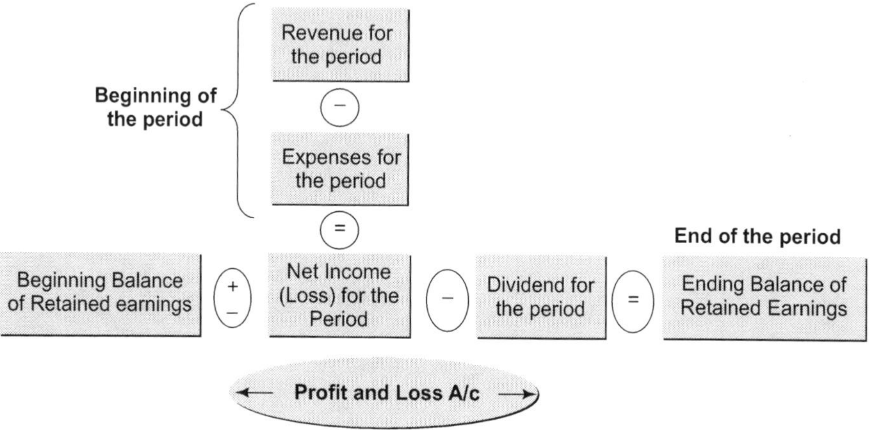

Figure 5.1 ***Balance Sheet and Profit and Loss Account Relation***

One can clearly make out that equations (5), (6) and (7) convey the same information in different ways. Let us now discuss the role of balance sheet items in generating the income statement.

The profit and loss account measures the income generated by the entity. The income is generated from or with the use of its assets. Thus, the profit and loss account measures and includes the revenue and income (which are part of the profit and loss account) arising out of assets (which form part of the balance sheet). Below, we uncover the essence of the requirement of the income statement again.

Need for an Income Statement

Normally, most of the events and transactions affect the assets and/or liabilities and hence affect the balance sheet. A change in the owner(s)' equity can either be brought about by a change in the owners' contribution or by sale transactions. Usually, the transaction of sale of goods and services has a two-way impact on the position of the entity.

- First, an asset increases, leading to an increase in the owners' equity. For example, by way of collecting money from the customers in a grocery shop.
- Second, an asset decreases, leading to a decrease in the owners' equity, such as, by way of delivery of the products by the grocery shop.

Therefore, subject to changes in the owners' contribution, the comparison of the owner(s)' equity between two periods will show the change in the owner(s)' equity affected by retained earnings. This does not provide much knowledge about the operations of the business (say, in terms of size, profitability of the business, etc.). Hence, in order to meet the information requirement, we summarized these transactions relating to revenue and expenses separately as income statement.

We should also note that revenue and expenses relate to a period (an accounting period), and not to a point in time, like assets and liabilities. Recognition and measurement of the revenue and expense are based on the ideas of realization, accrual and matching. Therefore, the income across an accounting period may be compared with the help of the data obtained from the profit and loss account.

Figure 5.2 gives us a peek into the corporate world. It links the income statement of Hindustan Unilever Limited (HUL) for the accounting period starting from April 2011 to March 2012, with the balance sheets of April 2011 and March 2012. At the start of the financial year (FY) of 2012, HUL had reserves and surplus balance at ₹ 25,190 million. The performance of HUL in FY2012 added ₹ 9,459 million to its reserve and surplus increasing it to ₹ 34,649 million as on March 2012.(Refer to Chapter 8, pg. 76 of *How to Read a Balance Sheet-Second Edition* for going through the Balance Sheet statement of HUL during the mentioned period).

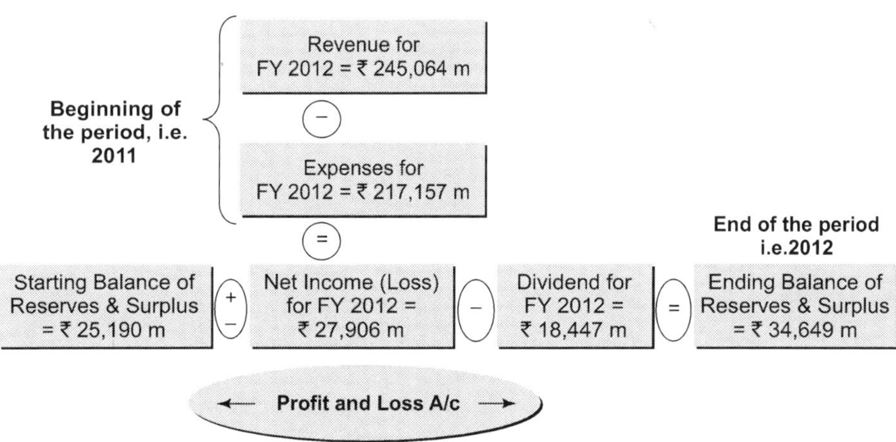

Figure 5.2 ***Hindustan Unilever Limited Income Statement FY2011-2012 and its Relation with Balance Sheets FY2011-2012 (all figures in Million)***

Now that we are pretty clear about the profit and loss statcment and its relevance with regards to the balance sheet, let us look at some of the more relevant items of the balance sheet and their treatment in the coming chapters.

6

CHAPTER

Inventory Valuation

The only thing certain with respect to prices is that they are not certain. This makes the process of recording inventory complex. There may be situations wherein the price at which we buy and record goods may not remain the same over a period of time, resulting in complications with respect to their carrying cost. For example, a company may buy 200 kg of cotton at ₹ 5 per kg and hence record it at ₹ 1,000. Eventually, the price of cotton may rise to say, ₹ 10. Now, this presents a dilemma, whether to record it at ₹ 1,000 (₹ 5 per kg) or ₹ 2,000 (₹ 10 per kg). Finding the exact price at which they need to be recorded becomes difficult.

These issues make it necessary to evolve a uniform approach for charging the cost of materials sold. Hence, the rule followed is that the inventory is usually recorded and charged to the profit and loss account on the basis of its historical cost, i.e., the price at which it is originally purchased.[11] While it solves a part of the problem, still some room for confusion remains in real life as there are situations wherein different quantities of the same good are purchased at different prices at different points in time. To get through this problem, there are four inventory valuation options at our disposal.

First In First Out (FIFO)

This is one of the most common systems of recording inventory. It assumes that the sales are made in the order at which they are purchased. The practical implication of this principle is as follows. Suppose that different quantities of a good (say, a liquid commodity such as lubricant oil) are purchased at different

[11] Rule for inventory valuation is lower of 'current market price' and the 'historical purchase price'. This is an example of conservative principle of accounting; and the conservative nature of accountants. To explain briefly, historical cost is the cash or equivalent, actually paid. Historical cost is ordinarily adjusted subsequently for the decrease in the economic utility/life of the item.

prices—The first 200 liters at ₹ 10 per liter; the next 500 liters at ₹ 15 per liter; and the next 300 liters at ₹ 20 per liter. Assume the entire purchase was stored in one tank. We have purchased a total of 1,000 liters of goods, each recorded at different prices. The total amount at which the inventory would be recorded is as follows:

(200 liters× ₹ 10 per liter) + (500 liters × ₹ 15 per liter) + (300 liters × ₹ 20 per liter) = ₹ 15,500.

Suppose 400 liters of this particular good is sold during the same accounting period. Now, this presents a problem. How do we find out as to which part of the above 1,000 liters of the good is sold? Quite logically, since the entire inventory was kept at one place with no clear separation, one would not be able to exactly pinpoint which portion of the inventory is sold. Hence, this situation would demand that we make certain assumptions. In the case of First In First Out (FIFO), we assume that the good (herein, lubricant oil) that is bought first will be the one which will be sold first.

In the above example, if we sell 400 liters of the good in question, then we will suppose that 200 liters of good bought at ₹ 10 per liter and 200 liters of good bought at ₹ 15 per liter are the ones that have been sold. So, the inventory left with us would be:

(300 liters × ₹ 15 per liter) + (300 liters × ₹ 20 per liter) = ₹ 10,500

A completely opposite assumption is made in the case of Last In First Out (LIFO).

Last In First Out (LIFO)

This is an alternative way of recording inventory. Companies following this principle assume that 'the goods which are bought last will be the one which will be sold first'. Let us straightaway move into the example being discussed to understand this principle. The inventory of the business was as follows:

(200 liters × ₹ 10 per liter) + (500 liters × ₹ 15 per liter) + (300 liters × 20 per liter) = ₹ 15,500

A business following this principle would assume that out of the 1000 liters, the portion of goods sold would be 300 liters bought at ₹ 20 per liter and 100 liters bought at ₹ 15 per liter. So, the inventory left with the business would be:

(200 liters × ₹ 10 per liter) + (400 liters × ₹ 15 per liter) = ₹ 8,000

In this case, we see that inventory levels have fallen down to ₹ 8,000.

One can observe how choosing different inventory valuation methods (FIFO, LIFO, or WAC, which we will study next) changes a company's cost of good sold and ending inventory position.

Weighted Average Cost (WAC)

Another possibility is to recalculate the cost of materials on a weighted average basis, after each purchase and sale. In this case, the inventory is recorded on the 'weighted average cost' (WAC). Again going back to the same example, the total purchase was:

(200 liters× ₹ 10 per liter) + (500 liters × ₹ 15 per liter) + (300 liters × 20 per liter) = ₹ 15,500

Now, the company has a total of 1000 liters of goods costing ₹ 15,500. The company will simply calculate the weighted average price of each liter of the good and assume it to be the cost of the inventory for future references. To illustrate, in this case, the cost of each inventory would be:

₹ 15,500 ÷ 1000 liters = ₹ 15.50 per liter

In our example of a sale of 400 liters, the balance inventory remaining with this company would be valued at:

600 liters × ₹ 15.50 = ₹ 9,300

Finnova: Hey Bholu! I can see you feeling sleepy. So, let me ask you a question. On 1st January, a bullion merchant started a business with cash worth ₹ 26 million. On 12th January and 25th January he purchases one kilogram of Gold (each day) for ₹ 12 million and ₹ 14 million respectively. On 31st January, he makes a sale of one kilogram of Gold for ₹ 15 million. Now compute his profit for the period using FIFO, WAC, and LIFO methods of inventory valuation.

Bholuram: I am fully awake. And please do not ask me such easy questions. Sales for the period would be ₹ 15 million. The cost of sales using FIFO, WAC and LIFO methods would be on ₹ 12 million, ₹ 13 million, and ₹ 14 million respectively. So the trading income for our bullion merchant would be ₹ 3 million using methods, ₹ 2 million using WAC method and ₹ 1 million using LIFO method.

Finnova: This is too much! You have made my day.

Bholuram: By the way, yesterday, my wife purchased some diamond-studded gold Jewellery from a big showroom. I was wondering what 'inventory valuation' method would the jewellery shop be using. Any help from your end.

Finnova: Where the inventory items are small in number (such as showroom with few goods) or not-interchangeable, they make use of a inventory valuation method known as 'simple identification method'. This is done using RFID tags i.e., Radio Frequency Identification technology. Thus, it is also a method to be used by the Jewellery showroom. Read on for some other relevant and interesting ... ☺

Specific Identification Method (SIM)

Specific identification of cost means that specific costs are applied to identify items of inventory being consumed. The total of various costs of the remaining stock identified constitutes the value of the inventory. This method of valuation is helpful in organizations handling a small number of items. It is also used where products are not interchangeable (i.e., one type of good/ product cannot be converted to another good/product). This is done by using RFID tags i.e., Radio Frequency Identification technology.

Most large retail giants such as Wal-Mart and Pantaloons have recognized the potential advantages for controlling inventory using RFID tags. Thus, they make use of 'Specific Identification' method of inventory valuation.

We now move on to a more comprehensive example to understand the treatment of inventory across the first three methods. We take the help of tables to illustrate how the cost of inventory changes with each purchase and sale transaction.

We now move on to a more comprehensive example to understand the treatment of inventory across these three methods. We take the help of tables to illustrate how the cost of inventory changes with each purchase and sale transaction.

Example 5: Ismail Traders

Table 6.1 shows purchase and sale transactions of Ismail Traders, traders of a particular commodity, during January 2014.

Table 6.1 ***Computation of Profit by FIFO, LIFO and WAC Methods***

Purchases				
Date	**Particulars**	**No. of units**	**Price per unit**	**Amount**
1 Jan '14	Inventory	500	3	1,500
5 Jan '14	Purchase	1,000	4	4,000
10 Jan '14	Purchase	2,000	5	10,000
15 Jan '14	Purchase	1,000	6	6,000
20 Jan '14	Purchase	3,000	4	12,000
25 Jan '14	Purchase	2,000	7	14,000
	Total	**9,500**		**47,500**

Sales				
Date	**Particulars**	**No. of units**	**Price per unit**	**Amount**
11 Jan '14	Sales	1,000		
14 Jan '14	Sales	500		
16 Jan '14	Sales	1,000		
21 Jan '14	Sales	2,000		
30 Jan '14	Sales	1,500		
	Total	**6,000**		
31 Jan '14	**Inventory**	**3,500**		

Recognition of the cost of goods sold and inventory valuation on the basis of first in first out (FIFO) is shown in Table 6.2.

The recognition of cost of goods sold and inventory valuation using the last in first out (LIFO) method is shown in Table 6.3.

Table 6.4 demonstrates the recognition of cost of goods sold and the inventory valuation using the weighted average cost (WAC) method.

Table 6.5 shows the comparison of the results using the three different valuation methods as a basis of recognition of the cost of goods sold and inventory.

From the illustration, we find that the purchase cost is the same irrespective of the method of inventory valuation. However, the cost of goods sold and the value of inventory at the end of the period are different for the three different methods of inventory valuation. If we use FIFO, the cost of goods sold, which is based on the prices of inventory procured earliest, prior to sales, would amount to ₹ 27,500. And the closing inventory of ₹ 3,500

Table 6.2 ***Ismail Traders: Inventory and Cost of Goods Sold under FIFO (all monetary figures in ₹)***

	Purchases			Sales			Inventory		
Date	**No. of units**	**Price per unit**	**Amount**	**No. of units**	**Price per unit**	**Amount**	**Price per unit**	**No. of units**	**Price per unit**
1 Jan 14	500	3	1,500						
5 Jan 14	1,000	4	4,000						
10 Jan 14	2,000	5	10,000						
11 Jan 14				500	3	1,500	500	4	2,000
				500	4	2,000	2,000	5	10,000
14 Jan 14				500	4	2,000	2,000	5	10,000
15 Jan 14	1,000	6	6,000				2,000 1,000	5 6	10,000 6,000
16 Jan 14				1,000	5	5,000	1,000 1,000	5 6	5,000 6,000
20 Jan 14	3,000	4	12,000				1,000 1,000 3,000	5 6 4	5,000 6,000 12,000
21 Jan 14				1,000	5	5,000			
				1,000	6	6,000	3,000	4	12,000
25 Jan 14	2,000	7	14,000				3,000 2,000	4 7	12,000 14,000
30 Jan 14				1,500	4	6,000	1,500 2,000	4 7	6,000 14,000
Total	**9,500**		**47,500**	**6,000**		**27,500**	**3,500**		**20,000**

Table 6.3 ***Ismail Traders: Inventory and Cost of Goods Sold under LIFO (all monetary figures in ₹)***

	Purchases			Sales			Inventory		
Date	**No. of units**	**Price per unit**	**Amount**	**No. of units**	**Price per unit**	**Amount**	**No. of units**	**Price per unit**	**Amount**
1 Jan 14	500	3	1,500						
5 Jan 14	1,000	4	4,000						
10 Jan 14	2,000	5	10,000						
11 Jan 14				1,000	5	5,000	500 1,000 1000	3 4 5	1,500 4,000 5,000
14 Jan 14				500	5	2,500	500 1,000 500	3 4 5	1,500 4,000 2,500
15 Jan 14	1,000	6	6,000				500 1,000 500 1000	3 4 5 6	1,500 4,000 2,500 6,000
16 Jan 14				1,000	6	6,000	500 1,000 500	3 4 5	1,500 4,000 2,500

(*Contd.*)

Table 6.3 ***(Contd.)***

Date	Purchases			Sales			Inventory		
	No. of units	**Price per unit**	**Amount**	**No. of units**	**Price per unit**	**Amount**	**No. of units**	**Price per unit**	**Amount**
20 Jan 14	3,000	4	12,000				500 1,000 500 3,000	3 4 5 4	1,500 4,000 2,500 12,000
21 Jan 14				2,000	4	8,000	500 1,000 500 1000	3 4 5 4	1,500 4,000 2,500 4,000
25 Jan 14	2,000	7	14,000				500 1,000 500 1000 2,000	3 4 5 4 7	1,500 4,000 2,500 4,000 14,000
30 Jan 14				1,500	7	10,500	500 1,000 500 1,000 500	3 4 5 4 7	1,500 4,000 2,500 4,000 3,500
Total	**9,500**		**47,500**	**6,000**		**32,000**	**3,500**		**15,500**

Table 6.4 ***Ismail Traders: Inventory and Cost of Goods Sold under WAC (all monetary figures in ₹)***

	Purchases			Sales			Inventory		
Date	**No. of units**	**Price per unit**	**Amount**	**No. of units**	**Price per unit**	**Amount**	**No. of units**	**Price per unit**	**Amount**
1 Jan 14	500	3	1,500				500	3	1,500
5 Jan 14	1,000	4	4,000				1,500		5,500
10 Jan 14	2,000	5	10,000				3,500	4,429	15,500
11 Jan 14				1,000	4,429	4,429	2,500	4,429	11,071
14 Jan 14				500	4,429	2,215	2,000	4,429	8,857
15 Jan 14	1,000	6	6,000				3,000	4,952	14857
16 Jan 14				1,000	4,952	4,952	2,000	4,952	9,905
20 Jan 14	3,000	4	12,000				5,000	4,381	21,905
21 Jan 14				2,000	4,381	8,762	3,000	4,381	13,143
25 Jan 14	2,000	7	14,000				5,000	5,4286	27,143
30 Jan 14				1,500	54,286	8,142	3,500	54,286	19,000
Total	**9,500**		**47,500**	**6,000**		**28,500**	**3,500**		**19,000**

Table 6.5 Ismail Traders: Inventory and Cost of Goods Sold under FIFO, LIFO and WAC (all figures in ₹)

Valuation method	Purchase cost	Cost of goods sold	Value of Inventory
FIFO	47,500	27,500	20,000
LIFO	47,500	32,000	15,500
WAC	47,500	28,500	19,000

units will be valued at ₹ 20,000, representing the most current purchase prices.

In the case of LIFO, we find that the cost of goods sold, which is based on the most recent prices of the inventory purchased, is ₹ 32,000. The closing inventory is valued at the prices of the earlier purchases at ₹ 19,000. In the case of WAC, we find that the cost of goods sold, which is based on the weighted average price of the inventory purchased, is ₹ 28,500. Closing inventory is also valued at the weighted average price of ₹ 15,500. In all the cases, inventory *plus* cost of goods sold would amount to the same, i.e., ₹ 47,500, since they are all based on the actual historical cost only.

Here again, over the entire life of the entity, there will be no difference, irrespective of the method used in the valuation of the cost of goods sold. There will also be no difference if the entire inventory is sold. *The inventory valuation differences reflect the effects of accounting periods on income measurement.* It is also easy to recognize the fact that, if the business purchases its entire inventory at the same prices, then the choice of inventory valuation method will have no relevance and the cost of goods sold and inventory would be same for all the three methods.

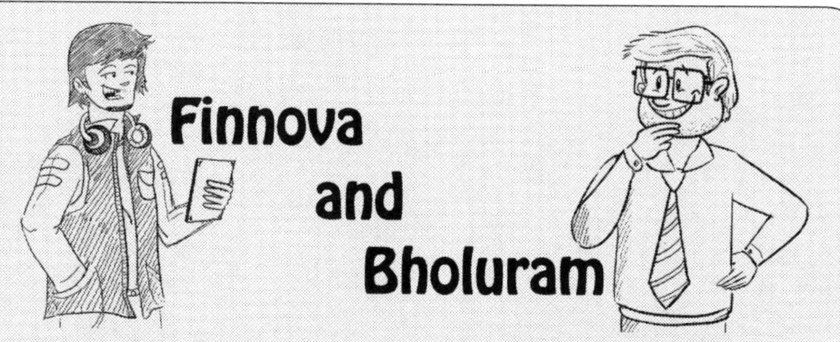

Bholuram: Stop Stop Finnova!! You have really enlightened me, but I have a question. Very often I have come across the word "stock taking". What does this mean?

Finnova: Excellent observation Bholu. Let me explain this with an example.

"Stock Taking" is a process wherein the physical inventory is taken of everything in the store periodically (usually, at the end of accounting periods). The principle for the inventory valuation is cost or market price, whichever is lower. It is done on a periodical basis while the year-end inventory valuation is done on the last week of the financial year. If suppose the "stock taking" is done on 25th March, and the accounting year ends on 31st March, then there needs to be adjustment of purchases and sales done between 26th March and 31st March. The adjustments of the goods must be on the basis of cost.

Let me explain using an example:

Stock Taken date – 26th March

Year-end date – 31st March

Actual stock on 26th March-	₹ 75,000
Purchases & Sales during 27-31st March	
Purchases –	₹ 15,000
Sales –	₹ 25,000

The sales are always with a margin of 25% on cost.

The stock computation as on 31st March would be:

Stock ascertained on 26th March -	₹ 75,000
Add: Purchases during 27-31st March -	₹ 15,000
	₹ 90,000
Less: Cost of goods sold during 27-31st March	
(25000 × 100/125)	₹ 20,000
Stock as on 31st March	₹ 70,000

Hence, the stock taken at the end of 31st March would be ₹ 70,000 (as shown above).

Bholuram: Hey, Finnova, considering if a raw material cost is ₹ 100 per unit, I buy 10 units of raw material, value of my raw material inventory is ₹ 1000/- (10×100), now if the Market Price of Raw material decreases to let say ₹ 90 per unit then, Value of my Raw material inventory will be ₹ 900/- (90×10, i.e. ₹ 100/- [1000-900] loss in my raw material inventory). Am I correct??

Finnova: Spot On ... Bhai Bhola!

Bholuram: Hm, ok, got it. But, how will this decrease in the raw material cost affect my cost of finished goods (considering I did not purchase any new raw material at ₹ 90 per unit and used the existing stock only which was purchased at ₹ 100 per unit)?

Finnova: I would like to answer this query in two parts:

- Theoretical reflection: These changes need not reflect exactly at the instant of the event (and thus in the same accounting period ... the P&L Statement figures and their item wise details may differ). However, you will also agree that in the long run i.e., if we club a few accounting periods together, these changes in the value of inventory will get captured.
- Practically how it happens: Changes in prices of raw material inventory, work in progress inventory, finished goods inventory, spares & supplies inventory are normally clubbed together and reflected as one item. For more on this I suggest you to go through a decent book on 'accounting of manufacturing entities'.

Bholuram: Thank you Finnova. This bit of clarification helps ☺

As a result of the above discussion, we can say that –Every firm, to value its 'inventory' and 'cost of goods sold' must decide on an inventory cost flow assumption. Accounting principles allow a company to specifically identify the cost of each of the items sold (i.e., the fourth method discussed above) or make an inventory cost flow assumption of FIFO, LIFO or weighted average cost (i.e., the first three methods discussed above). Please note that the physical flow of inventory need not exactly imitate the cost flow, but the inventory cost flow method chosen should be the one that best reflects the firm's working.

7

CHAPTER

Income Statement of a Manufacturing Concern

Based on the earlier chapters, one can deduce that the profit and loss account incorporates all the revenue and expense transactions relating to business operations. It has been observed that the process of business operations is more complex in manufacturing firms and hence, this demands the preparation of a slightly extended version of the profit and loss account. For example, a manufacturing firm often has four types of inventory, namely – *raw material* inventory, *work-in-progress* inventory, *finished goods* inventory, and *supplies & spares* inventory. Consequently, in a manufacturing concern, the profit and loss account can be divided into four parts, i.e., the 'manufacturing account', 'trading account', 'profit and loss account' and 'profit and loss appropriation account'. These accounts can be understood as follows:

Manufacturing Account

During a given accounting period, the manufacturing account provides us with the cost of goods manufactured by the manufacturer. This is the reason why many organizations that do not perform manufacturing operations, do not prepare this account. For example, M/s Rasik lal Daruwala & Co. is a manufacturer of sports goods. For the year ended March 31, 2013, the following transactions took place:

• Raw material purchased	₹ 60,000
• Productivewages	₹ 20,000
• Powerandfuelconsumed	₹ 10,000
• Rentoffactory	₹ 5,000

It is also known that there was a stock (inventory) of work-in-progress as on the beginning of the year, amounting to ₹ 40,000 and the closing stock of work-in-progress is ₹ 10,000. The opening and closing stocks of raw material were ₹ 5,000 and ₹ 15,000 respectively.

In the above case, the manufacturing account of M/s Rasik lal Daruwala & Co. shall be as follows:

Table 7.1 ***Manufacturing Account of M/s Rasik lal Daruwala & Co. for thehe Year Ended March 31, 2013 (All figures in ₹)***

Debit		Credit	
Particulars	**Amount**	**Particulars**	**Amount**
Opening work-in-progress	40,000	Closing work-in-progress	10,000
Raw material consumed: Opening stock 5,000 Add: Purchases 60,000 Less: Closing stock (15,000)		Cost of production for the period transferred to the trading account	115,000
Productive wages	50,000		
Power and fuel	20,000		
Factory rent	10,000		
	5,000		
Total	**125,000**	**Total**	**125,000**

In the above manufacturing account, the cost of manufacturing associated with the carried forward inventory is represented by opening work-in-progress (WIP). The current year's manufacturing cost is added to the opening WIP, i.e., raw materials consumed, productive wages, fuel and rent costs. Finally, the manufacturing cost of closing work-in-progress with respect to the inventory unsold and carried forward to the next year is subtracted to give us the current year's cost of production.

Continuing with the illustration of M/s Rasik lal Daruwala & Co., we move to the trading account.

Trading Account

The *trading account* indicates the amount of gross profit earned by the business, by matching the cost of the sales with the revenues generated by the business during the period. In many cases, the manufacturing account is merged with the trading account to give us a combined manufacturing and trading account. In the case of a manufacturer who is also a trader, the trading account discloses not only the profit made by the business by selling the manufactured goods, but also profits generated by the sale of goods purchased directly from others. Continuing with the same example, we are given the following additional information:

• Openingstock (finished goods)	₹ 25,000
• Sale	₹ 160,000
• Closingstock (finished goods)	₹ 35,000
• Cartage	₹ 15,000
• Purchase (finished goods)	₹ 15,000

Based on the above information, the trading account of the firm appears as shown in Table 7.2.

Table 7.2 ***Trading Account of M/s Rasik lal & Co. for the Year Ended March 31, 2013 (All figures in ₹)***

Debit		Credit	
Particulars Amount	**Amount**	**Particulars Amount**	**Amount**
		Sales	16,000
Opening finished goods	25,000	Closing stock of finished goods	35,000
Cost of production for the period transferred from manufacturing account	115,000		
Purchase of finished goods	15,000		
Cartage expenses	15,000		
Gross profit	25,000		
Total	**195,000**	**Total**	**195,000**

In this way, one can calculate the amount of gross profit earned by matching the cost of sales with the revenues generated by the business. In Table 7.2, the cost of sales (₹ 170,000) is subtracted from the revenues generated (₹ 195,000) to give us the gross profit (₹ 25,000) as a balancing figure.

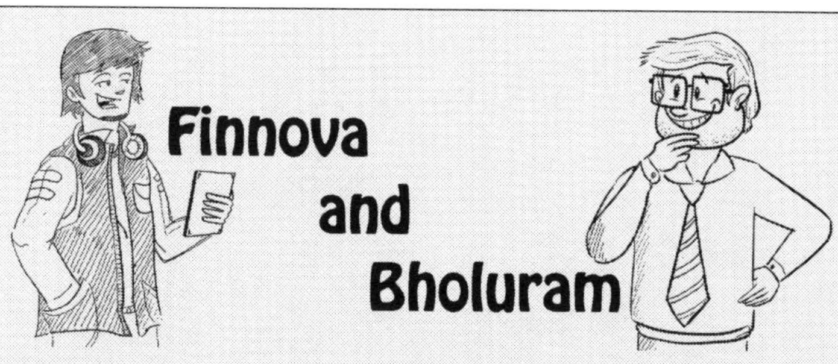

Bholuram: Hey Finnova, I have a confusion. Why do you keep adding the year's opening figures in the current year's cost of production (example,opening stock of raw materials) and subtracting the closing figures (example, closing stock of raw materials) to get the current year's figures?

Finnova: Bhola, let me explain this concept with a simple example. Suppose, you are in the business of selling apples. Now on Monday you took 20 apples from your house to sell them in your shop, but are able to sell only 15. You leave the remaining five apples in your shop. On Tuesday, you again take 20 apples from your house to the market. At the end of the day you make a count and find that you are left with seven apples in your shop.

Now, imagine the apples left on Monday as the Opening stock (5), the apples taken from your house to the shop on Tuesday (20) as the goods produced in the current year and the apples left at the end of Tuesday (7) as the Closing Stock. Now, if we need to calculate the cost of goods sold in the current period, i.e. the number of apples sold on Tuesday. To do so, you will first calculate the total number of apples that you had at your disposal for potential sales on Tuesday. To arrive at this figure, you will add the apples left at the end of Monday with the apples brought to the shop on Tuesday, i.e., 5 + 20 = 25 apples. This gives us the maximum number of apples that were available to us for sale, i.e., this gives us the 'goods available for sale'. Now, we simply subtract the closing stock, i.e., the number of apples left at the end of Tuesday to give us the number of apples actually sold on Tuesday, i.e., (25 – 7) = 18 apples. This corresponds to the goods sold during the period.

The same concept is applied in case of accounts wherein the previous year's closing figure is added to the current year's production figure and the current year's closing figure is subtracted from the obtained total to give us the current year's cost figures.

Table 7.3 ***Common-Size 'Income Statement' Figures of Three Indian Companies (all figures in ₹ crores)***

	Raymond Limited		Reliance Industries Ltd.		Infosys Limited	
Financial Year ⇒	**2013**	**2012**	**2013**	**2012**	**2013**	**2012**
Sales / Income From Operations	4,087	3,657	397,062	358,501	40,352	33,734
Less: Cost of Goods Sold	2,357	1,983	332,250	298,191	26,310	20,893
Gross Profit	1,730	1,674	64,812	60,310	14,042	12,841
Less: Sales, General & Administration Expenses	1,341	1,198	31,767	25,493	2,424	2,118
EBIDTA (Earnings Before Interest, Depreciation, Taxes & Amortization)	**389**	**476**	**33,045**	**34,817**	**11,618**	**10,723**
Less: Depreciation & Amortization Expenses	189	166	11,232	12,401	1,099	928
Operating Profit	200	310	21,813	22,416	10,519	9,795
Adjusted for Other Income & Similar Items	74	72	7,860	6,201	2,365	1,904
Adjusted for Exceptional Items	(29)	-	-	(309)	(85)	-
EBIT (Earnings Before Interest Tax)	245	382	29,673	28,308	12,799	11,699
Less: Interest Expenses & Financial Charges	191	165	3,463	2,893	-	-
EBT (Earnings Before Tax, also known as, Profit Before Tax i.e., PBT)	**54**	**217**	**26,210**	**25,415**	**12,799**	**11,699**
Less: Corporate Income Tax Expenses	25	61	5,331	5,691	3,370	3,367
Net Profit (also, Profit After Tax i.e., PAT)	**29**	**156**	**20,879**	**19,724**	**9,429**	**8,332**
No. of Shares (from Balance Sheet)	6	6	294	294	57	57
Earnings Per Share (EPS)	4.68	25.42	71.11	67.18	165.02	145.82

Once a manufacturing firm reaches this state, it goes on to compute its net income using the profit and loss account. The process of computing the ending balance of reserves and surplus, i.e., current period's closing retained earnings from a firm's net income figures is part of the *profit and loss appropriation account.* One can easily conclude that these two accounts—*profit and loss account* and *profit and loss appropriation account,* are common to all types of firms, i.e., manufacturing or otherwise.

In Table 7.3 in page 66, we see a live example of three well known companies in varied lines of business together in line, comparing each other's financial strengths and weakness on an year-on-year basis.

If we look at the textile giant Raymond's numbers, we observe that its *income from operations* has risen from ₹ 3,657 crores in FY2012 to ₹ 4,087 crores in FY2013 (about ₹ 430 crores increase). On the other hand, conglomerate Reliance Industries'shas risen from ₹ 358,501 crores to ₹ 397,062 crores during this period (about ₹ 38,561 crores increase). Similar was the case with IT-biggie Infosys. Its *income from operations* has gone up by ₹ 6,618 crores i.e., from ₹ 33,734 cores to ₹ 40,352 crores during the same accounting period.

Now, if we focus at the *net profit figures in the illustration above,* we observe that Raymond's net profit has gone down from ₹ 156 crores in FY2012 to ₹ 29 in FY2013 (a fall of about ₹ 127 crores). The scenario is exactly different for the other two firms. Reliance Industries net income has gone up from ₹ 19,724 crores in FY2012 to ₹ 20,879 in FY2013 (about ₹ 1,155 crores increase). In the case of Infosys,the net profit figures have moved up by ₹ 1,097 crores i.e., they have gone up from ₹ 8,332 crores to ₹ 9,429 during this period.

All in all, Reliance Industries seems to be having a good time and an upper hand when it comes to profit earning. While, Raymond's seems to lag behind the other two companies on the basis of these figures. Readers would have also noted that these companies being from different industries are bound to have differing performance; some good and some not so good; largely reflecting the times they are going through. And that is what an income statement is largely intended to do.

8

CHAPTER

Possible Future Expenses

Another situation encountered by us, which poses some measurement difficulty, is where costs[12] are to be incurred in subsequent periods but which are directly in relation to the revenue of a given accounting period. These expenses pose an important problem since the expense is more or less certain, but the amount is by and large not certain. We normally estimate the amount of expense in question, relating to an accounting period, in order to make a reasonably accurate measurement of the profit or loss of the period. Examples of such expenses could be, not receiving payments (collection losses) with respect to credit sales (say, of telephone operators like Bharti Airtel, BSNL and Vodafone), which, may be known only in a future period. Warranty costs to be incurred with respect to sales of the period (say, of a durable consumer goods player like Samsung and Videocon Industries), which are to be incurred in future; and similar other cases including 'Product Guarantee-period costs'. An example of such a case, i.e., bad debt expense is subsequently discussed.

Bad Debt Expense

In most business situations, sale 'on credit' is common. We also treat such a sale as 'realized' since it produces a certain asset—accounts receivable. Thus, a credit sale is recognized at the point of sale, during the accounting period in which the transaction takes place. The uncollected balance at the close of the accounting period is reflected as an asset on the balance sheet commonly mentioned as *sundry debtors* or *accounts receivable* or *trade debtors*.

Now, if the customer is not able to make the payment, both these accounting records, i.e., record as revenue of the period and record as asset at the close of the period will amount to an overstatement in the

[12]Here, we refer to those costs that are to be incurred in subsequent periods, but are in relation to the revenue of this year (Matching Principle).

figures of sales and accounts receivable respectively. Thus, in an ideal scenario, accountants would deduct the total amount of bad debt (due to bad credit sales) from these two figures. However, accountants have no error-free basis of estimating the exact amount of such collection losses at the time of sale. You will concur that the existence and the exact amount of bad debts will be known only in a subsequent accounting period. This is the reason why accountants make an estimate of the default in this accounting period. Let us learn this through Example 6.

Example 6: Roshini Traders

A business is started in the name and style of 'Roshini Traders' with owner(s) equity of ₹ 2,500. The business makes four credit sales of ₹ 250 each, during an accounting period. The cost of sales for the same is known to be ₹ 125 each. The profit and loss account is shown in Table 8.1.

Table 8.1 ***Profit and Loss Account of Roshini Traders (for the accounting period)***

Expenses	₹	Revenues	₹
Cost of goods sold Profit for the period	500 500	Sales	1,000
Total	**1,000**	**Total**	**1,000**

The balance sheet records arising from this is shown in Table 8.2.

Table 8.2 ***Balance Sheet of Roshini Traders (as at the close of the accounting period)***

Assets	₹	Liabilities	₹
Accounts receivable Other assets	1,000 2,000	Retained earnings Owner(s)' contributed equity	500 2,500
Total	**3,000**	**Total**	**3,000**

The word 'bad' implies that an account receivable is no more recoverable. Thus, an amount that was supposed to be received in the future, but is not received and there is no chance of its recovery in its future is known as 'bad'. There could be varied reasons for the occurrence of bad debts, for example, closure of the buying party or a court order on the buyer, etc.

Now, assuming that in the above example, one of the accounts goes bad, then the collection loss will amount to ₹ 250. Now if we do not take the fact of one credit sale worth ₹ 250 going bad then we would have overstated the receivables (asset in the balance sheet), sales (revenue in the profit and loss account) and profits (retained earnings in the balance sheet). While it is not possible to arrive at a certain bad debt figure before hand, it is possible for us to make a rough estimation of the losses on account of *bad debts*, and reduce the revenues and thereby, profits to that extent.

This is achieved by recognizing this amount of ₹ 250 as an increase in the expense—*bad debts expense*, thereby, reducing profit. Thus, we will have a profit and loss account and a balance sheet as shown in Table 8.3 and Table 8.4 below.

Table 8.3 ***Profit and Loss Account of Roshini Traders (For the accounting period)***

Expenses	₹	**Revenues**	₹
Cost of goods sold	500	Sales	1,000
Bad debt expense	250		
Profit for the period	250		
Total	**1,000**	**Total**	**1,000**

Table 8.4 ***Balance Sheet of Roshini Traders (As at the close of the accounting period)***

Assets	₹	**Revenues**	₹
Accounts receivable 1,000		Retained earnings	250
Less: Estimated collection loss (250)	750		
Other assets	2,000	Other equities	2,500
Total	**2,750**	**Total**	**2,750**

Note that in the example, Roshini Traders has estimated its bad debts to be ₹ 250. However, it may or may not turn out to be the case in the next accounting period. Generally, the probable collection losses are estimated and provided for by charging them as an expense of the period. Such an estimated expense is reduced from the value of the asset; accounts receivable, to show the realizable value of the asset.

9

CHAPTER

Depreciation, Amortization and Depletion

Every asset used in the business has a limited useful life. The *useful life* is the period of time for which an asset can be economically used. This implies that the benefits from the particular asset will be enjoyed by the organization only during its useful life, after which the asset would become incapable to be put to any profitable use. In the next two paragraphs, we provide two different explanations for adjusting this.

In our discussion earlier, we have seen that fixed assets are long lived and provide benefits beyond one operating cycle. While discussing the idea of expense, we saw that expenses are expired costs. All costs incurred on any asset with a limited life, thus, expire during its lifetime. Using this understanding, it is not difficult to perceive what depreciation is. *Depreciation expense* is the expired cost of an asset during an accounting period. Thus, depreciation is that part of the fixed asset which in a sense has been *used up* by the company to generate the current year's revenue.

For a firm, the value of the asset does not remain the same throughout the life of the asset. It is reduced throughout the life of an asset as a result of the wear and tear that it undergoes, as a result of constant use. Quite obviously, no one would put the same value to a brand new car and a car which, let us say, is 10 years old. So, in order to represent a true and accurate value of the asset, the amount at which the asset is recorded in the balance sheet is reduced in proportion to the life of the asset. The older the asset, the more is the reduction in value. Such reduction in value is referred to as *depreciation*.

Thus, depreciation may also be defined as the *reduction in value of an asset as a result of the wear and tear due to use or with passing of time.* (Please read through Chapter 3 of *How to Read a Balance Sheet –Second Edition*).

Let us illustrate this idea with Example 7.

Example 7: Manoj Joshi

Manoj Joshi purchased a sewing machine having a five-year life and no salvage value for ₹ 5,000 for his tailoring business. During the life of the asset, it will be able to earn revenue of ₹ 10,000.

Assuming no other expenses, it is simple arithmetic to figure out that by using the machine, we make a profit of ₹ 5,000 over its lifetime i.e. ₹ 10,000 revenues less ₹ 5,000 for cost of the machine. The problem of depreciation arises when we have to measure the profits annually. What should be the amount of profit to be recognized each year?

We can approach this problem by using Table 9.1. Assume that the following scale shows the amount of revenue earned. We take it that the revenue is earned in equal amounts during the five years of the life of the asset.

Table 9.1 ***Manoj Joshi, Revenue over the Period of Use of the Assets (All figures in ₹)***

Total revenue						**= ₹ 10,000**
Period →	1	2	3	4	5	
Amount	2,000	2,000	2,000	2,000	2,000	= ₹ 10,000

Assuming no other costs, we can say that the only cost is the cost of the sewing machine, which becomes an expense over the five-year period, since there is no salvage value. Now, the question is, how should we apportion this cost over the five-year life of the asset?

If we make the simple assumption that the cost expires in an equal proportion, we have this simplest solution as shown in Table 9.2.

Now, having made the assumption of spreading the cost equally, we have come to the conclusion that one-fifth of the cost of the asset expires annually.

Table 9.2 ***Manoj Joshi, Cost Expiration over the Period of Use of the Assets (All figures in ₹)***

Total machine cost						**= ₹ 5,000**
Period →	1	2	3	4	5	
Amount	1,000	1,000	1,000	1,000	1,000	= ₹ 5,000
Unexpired at the end of the period	4,000	3,000	2,000	1,000	0	

That portion of the cost of the asset, which is reckoned to expire during an accounting period, is what is termed as *depreciation expense*. This also clarifies that, normally, the total amount of depreciation on the asset shall not be more than the depreciable cost of the asset. It is this 'expense' which is matched against the revenues of a period, for determining the profit.

From Example 7, based on the assumptions made, we can easily determine that the profit per annum is ₹ 1,000, i.e., ₹ 5,000 over the useful life of the asset. To recapitulate, *depreciation expense* is the cost of a fixed asset, written of or matched as expense against the revenues of the different periods during which the asset is used.

Bholuram: Hey Finnova, I have a query related to the items that remain idle for a long time or are not used after sometime due to new technology upgraded items or rather say equipments... :/

Finnova: You don't need to be formal, just go ahead and ask.

Bholuram: Should depreciation be provided on such fixed assets lying idle too?

Finnova: Bhola, the value of an asset depreciates not only by putting it to use, but also due to lapse of time or technology obsolescence. Thus, even an idle fixed asset should have depreciation.

Bholuram: You make things so simple for me.☺

Methods of Depreciation

In Example 7, we assumed that the cost of asset expires uniformly over its useful life. However, this assumption is not based on any theoretical construct. Therefore, it is possible for us to assume any other basis of expiration. The only theoretical basis for these assumptions could be that the entire cost less any salvage value, must expire over its useful life.

There are different methods for depreciation, which differ from one another only on the basis of how the cost should be treated as expiring over the life of the asset. Essentially, depreciation methods follow either of two broad approaches, the accelerated approach and the uniform approach. Methods in which larger amounts are expired during the initial years of the life of the assets are known as the accelerated methods of depreciation. This method has the backing of the principle of conservatism. The level of uncertainty is higher into the future and hence, expiration of the cost at the earliest is welcome. The other method tries to expire the cost uniformly over the useful life of the assets and hence, is considered to be the most easy to follow method. This is also the most popular method of depreciation. We shall brief discuss some of the most commonly used methods. However, in order to understand the methods, we should be clear about the following ideas:

Original Cost of the Asset

This is the cost incurred in making the asset available for use at the first instance. This amount is specified and known at the time of acquisition of the asset.

Salvage Value

This is the expected recovery or sales value of the asset at the end of its useful life. This value, in most cases, is not known and hence, needs to be estimated. When there is no certainty about the recoverable value at the end of an asset's useful life, it is prudent to assume a zero salvage value.

Useful Life

This is the expected time period for which the asset is to provide economic service. It is the period for which the asset can be used for production. This period also is not known with any certainty at the time when the asset is acquired. This is usually estimated on the basis of experience or technical factors.

Depreciable Cost

This is the original cost of the asset, less its salvage value. This is the amount of expense the enterprise will be incurring on account of the expired costs of the fixed asset over its useful or economic life.

Book Value

The written down value of the asset at any point of time, is its original cost, less depreciation to date (commonly known as, *accumulated depreciation*).

This is also referred to as the *written down value* or *remaining book value*. This is the value at which assets are recorded in the balance sheet.

While there are many ways to provide depreciation[13], we list the two most popular ones in Figure 9.1.

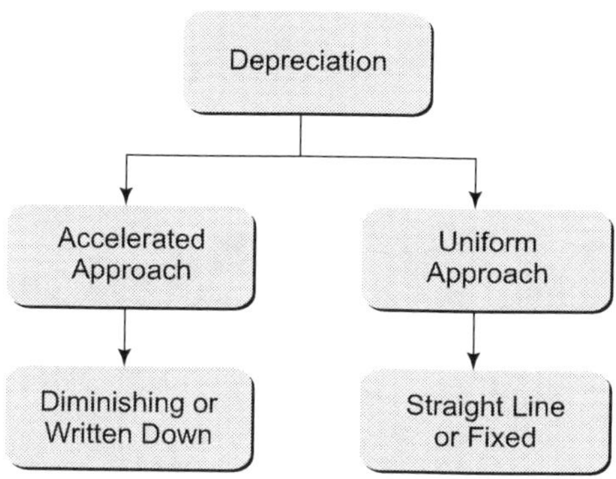

Figure 9.1 ***Depreciation Methods***

Straight Line/Fixed Method

Under this method, a fixed percentage of the *original cost* of the asset is depreciated each year till the asset value becomes nil. Let us understand the concept with the help of Example 8.

Example 8: Rahul Traders

Assume that Rahul Traders acquire a machine at the beginning of operations, at ₹ 10,000. It is expected that the machine will last 10 years and will have no salvage value at the end of its useful life. The machine needs to be depreciated using the straight line method of depreciation.

The assumption under the straight-line method is that the cost of the equipment expires uniformly over time[14]. The depreciation every year for the machine under the straight-line method will be 1/10 or 10 percent of the cost of the asset. Annual depreciation, therefore, will be ₹ 1,000 (being ₹ 10,000/10). The written down value at the end of the first year will be ₹ 10,000 *less* ₹ 1,000 = ₹ 9,000.

[13]The various methods of depreciation have already been discussed in the book *How to Read a Balance Sheet 2/e*.

[14]It works out to be depreciable cost divided by the estimated life of the asset. The depreciable cost is equal to the original cost of the equipment less its salvage value.

Since the depreciation will remain constant throughout the lifetime of the machine, the second year depreciation will also be ₹ 1,000 and at the end of the second year, the written down value of the machine will be ₹ 10,000 *less* (1,000 + 1,000) or (9,000 *less* 1,000) = ₹ 8,000, and so on. The book value will become zero at the end of 10 years. Table 9.3 shows the annual depreciation, accumulated depreciation and remaining book value of the asset during its useful life.

Table 9.3 ***Depreciation @ 10% Per Annum: Straight Line Method (all Amount in ₹)***

Year	Cost	Annual depreciation	Accumulated depreciation	Remaining book value
0	10,000			
1	10,000	1,000	1,000	9,000
2	10,000	1,000	2,000	8,000
3	10,000	1,000	3,000	7,000
4	10,000	1,000	4,000	6,000
5	10,000	1,000	5,000	5,000
6	10,000	1,000	6,000	4,000
7	10,000	1,000	7,000	3,000
8	10,000	1,000	8,000	2,000
9	10,000	1,000	9,000	1,000
10	10,000	1,000	10,000	0

The accumulated depreciation (total depreciation charged till date) will increase annually, at a uniform rate, becoming equal to the depreciable cost of the asset at the end of its useful life.

Diminishing Balance/Written Down Value Depreciation

Under the *written down value (W.D.V.) /diminishing balance / reducing balance method*, the depreciation for each year is calculated as a fixed percentage of the balance figure of the asset brought forward from the previous year. Depreciation is taken as a certain rate, and it is applied to the written down value of the asset as, at the beginning of each year. The effect of this method is that the amount of depreciation charged every year is an amount less than that in the previous year. This is due to the fact that the expiration reduces the value of the asset and the same rate of expiration is applied to the net value of the asset at the beginning of each year. This results in lower amounts of depreciation during successive years. The assumption is that the amount of expiration of the cost of the asset is higher during the initial years. (If you feel confused, then do not worry, a detailed example at the end of the section will make it clearer.)

In the WDV method, we need to decide on a depreciation rate in advance. Usually, it is taken to be twice the rate of straight-line depreciation[15]. We carry the example of Rahul Traders further to show the calculation of depreciation using the WDV Method at the rate of 20 percent.

The non-allocated portion of the cost is usually charged as depreciation in the last year of the life of the asset. Since there is no salvage value for the asset at the end of its useful life, the terminal year depreciation will be taken as ₹ 1,342, i.e., ₹ 268 (the depreciation for the period) plus ₹ 1074 (the terminal value of the asset).

Table 9.4 **Depreciation @ Down Value 20% Per Annum: Written Method (all Amount in ₹)**

Year	Original cost	Annual depreciation	Accumulated depreciation	Remaining book value
0	10,000			10,000
1	10,000	2,000	2,000	8,000
2	10,000	1,600	3,600	6,400
3	10,000	1,280	4,880	5,120
4	10,000	1,024	5,904	4,096
5	10,000	819	6,723	3,277
6	10,000	655	7,379	2,621
7	10,000	524	7,903	2,097
8	10,000	419	8,322	1,678
9	10,000	336	8,658	1,342
10	10,000	268	8,926	1,074

[15]One interesting observation to be made here is that while in the straight-line method of charging depreciation, the asset value will eventually reduce to zero; such a scenario is not at all possible in the diminishing balance method. This is because the depreciation is charged as a percentage of previous year figures and hence it will always be lower than the value of the asset. So, the question is, will not the asset ever cease to exist? To take care of such a problem, the remaining value of an asset is generally depreciated at a single go in its last year to bring its value down to zero and consequently remove it from the balance sheet. The remainder, at the end of the period, is considered to be the terminal depreciation (total cost of the asset *minus* depreciation charged till date) during the last year of the life of the asset, when no salvage value is expected. Otherwise the residual is considered as the salvage value.

Annual depreciation under the written down value method is the highest during the first year and goes on reducing over the subsequent years. However, the rate of decline reduces as the number of years approaches the end of the life of the asset. The accumulated depreciation, similarly, increases at a rapid rate during the initial years and the rate of increase declines in later years. The remaining book value of the asset is a declining curve.

Sum of the Year's Digit Method

Sum of the year's digit produces results akin to the written down value method, with the difference that there will be no residual left. This method applies a declining fraction to the depreciable cost of the asset. The declining fraction is constructed by taking the number of years of useful service left at the beginning of the year, as the numerator, and the sum of the digits of the number of years of useful life, as the denominator.

If we look at Table 9.5, then we find that if the asset has 10 years of useful life, the denominator of the fraction will be equal to (10+9+8+7+6+5+4+3+2+1) i.e. 55. So, the first year's depreciation charge will be 10/55, the second year's depreciation will be 9/55 and so on. Finally the last year's depreciation charge will be 1/55. Our illustration in Table 9.5 illustrates the annual depreciation and other items, using the sum-of-the-years digit method.

Table 9.5 ***Depreciation: Sum of the Years' Method (all Amount in ₹)***

Year	Original cost	Annual depreciation	Accumulated depreciation	Remaining book value
0	10,000			
1	10,000	1,818	1,818	8,182
2	10,000	1,636	3,455	6,545
3	10,000	1,455	4,909	5,091
4	10,000	1,273	6,182	3,818
5	10,000	1,091	7,273	2,727
6	10,000	909	8,182	1,818
7	10,000	727	8,909	1,091
8	10,000	545	9,455	545
9	10,000	364	9,818	182
10	10,000	182	10,000	0

Intangible Assets and Amortization

Several times, business enterprises acquire intangible long-term assets, such as patent rights, distribution rights or copyrights, by paying large sums of money. So, intangible assets also represent unexpired costs and need to be accounted for their decrease in the future economic utility accordingly. The method we use to slowly expire intangible assets is known as amortization. Hence, we can take amortization to mean the depreciation of the intangible assets.

Intangible assets are a lot more difficult to be identified or verified. So, in order to simplify their accounting, it is usual practice to amortize intangible assets on a straight-line basis. Since it is difficult to determine the useful life of intangible assets in many cases, they are amortized over a reasonably short period. This decision is irrespective of the fact that some of these intangible assets may have a much longer legal life.

Depletion

Another concept related to depreciation and amortization is *depletion. Depletion is applicable if* a company has some wasting asset, usually natural resources (oil reserve or mineral ore deposits). For example, a coal mine, wherein the asset value keeps on decreasing with use or passage of time. In such a case, the depreciation charged will be proportionate to the percentage of asset used up or wasted. For example, let us suppose a coal mine that has a 100,000 ton capacity and a value of ₹ 1,000,000. Then, if in the first year, a total of 15,000 ton of coal is mined, then the depreciation charged would be ₹ 1,000,000 × (15,000/100,000) = ₹ 150,000.

Depreciation and Profit Measurement

What we have learnt from discussion of the depreciation methods is that, depending on the method used for charging depreciation or recognition of expiration of the cost of the fixed assets, we have a different amount of charge for annual depreciation. It could also be noticed that over the entire life of the asset, the total amount of depreciation charge cannot be different from the depreciable cost of the asset. Thus, the difference is only in terms of the annual apportionment. The net effect of the methods is therefore, in terms of showing less or more profit in any particular year. This can be demonstrated by continuing with our earlier illustration.

Example 8: Rahul Traders...continued

Assume that the company using the machine in our earlier illustration earns ₹ 5,000 per annum in earnings before depreciation. The difference in the annual measurement of profit under the straight-line and written down value methods is illustrated in Table 9.6.

Table 9.6 ***Profit Measurement under Different Depreciation Methods (all figures in ₹)***

Year	Earnings before depreciation	Depreciation		Profit	
		Straight-line	W.D.V.	Straight-line	W.D.V.
0					
1	5,000	1,000	2,000	4,000	3,000
2	5,000	1,000	1,600	4,000	3,400
3	5,000	1,000	1,280	4,000	3,720
4	5,000	1,000	1,024	4,000	3,976
5	5,000	1,000	819	4,000	4,181
6	5,000	1,000	655	4,000	4,345
7	5,000	1,000	524	4,000	4,476
8	5,000	1,000	419	4,000	4,581
9	5,000	1,000	336	4,000	4,664
10	5,000	1,000	269+1,074[16]	4,000	3,657
Total	**50,000**	**10,000**	**10,000**	**40,000**	**40,000**

Table 9.6 and related discussion gives us some important insights. One of the important lessons is that any particular method of depreciation has no effect on the income measurement of the business over its entire life. However, different methods of depreciation will produce different profit figures on a year-to-year basis. It is not difficult to find an explanation for this variation.

Difference: Depreciation, Amortization and Depletion

Frequently, we come across the question of the differences between depreciation, amortization and depletion. We provide a summary in the Table 9.7 below.

[16] Includes the non-allocated depreciation charge of 1,074, since there is no salvage value for the fixed asset; under this method, there will always be a terminal unabsorbed depreciation. All figures are rounded off.

Table 9.7 ***Difference: Depreciation, Depletion and Amortization***

Depreciation	Depletion	Amortization
Depreciation is a measure of wearing out, consumption or other loss of value of a depreciable asset, arising from use, efflux ion of time or obsolescence through technology and market changes. It is allocated so as to charge a fair proportion in each accounting period, during the useful life of the asset. Depreciation expense is applicable on all tangible long-term assets, whose useful life is pre-determined. For example, the depreciation expense on movable and immovable machineries in a service industry, such as air cargo services.	*Depletion* charge is a measure of exhaustion of a wasting asset, represented by a periodic write-off of the cost or other substituted value. For example, depletion charge of using a mine of iron ore and coal, by a steel manufacturer owning those mines.	*Amortization* is the gradual and systematic writing-off of an intangible long-term asset over an appropriate period. For example, amortization of business restructuring expenses and software implementation expenses, by a large banking firm.

Bholuram: Finnova, there are three main methods of depreciation right.. but my question is, can a company use two methods of depreciation?

Finnova: Bhola...you are really a bholuram. Yes, most companies use two or more methods of depreciation...knowingly and it is acceptable for big companies to depreciate its plant assets by using the straight line method on its financial statements, lets say an IT firm would be depreciating its computers over ten years for its financial statements, while using an accelerated method on its income tax return, i.e. using seven years for its income tax return.

Bholuram: Oh! now I see. In that case, which is the most used depreciation method of all or rather which one is the best?

Finnova: See Bhola, when it comes to depreciation, it is done to match revenues and expenses. There may be times when a machine will be more productive in the early years and less productive in the later years. Here an accelerated method may be best.

But if we see the other side of the coin, i.e., accountants are expensive nowadays and the cost-benefit rule comes into play for a company, hence, most companies would want accountants to just use a straight-line method to keep things simple. So.... which method is the best... depends on lots of factors.

Bholuram: Hm...Fair enough ☺

Solved Illustrations

Example 1: Ram Software

Following are the few transactions for Ram Software Limited (RSL) for two periods:

1st Period:

- On March 1, Ram & others invest ₹ 50,000 in cash in RSL.
- On March 2, Ram took a loan of ₹ 20,000 from Venugopal for RSL. Being a nice friend,
- Being a nice friend, Venugopal does not demand any interest on the loan amount and asks it to be repaid in six months' time.
- On March 3, RSL purchased for cash two computers, each costing ₹ 29,000.
- On March 4, RSL purchased supplies especially stationary for ₹ 6,000 on credit.
- On March 19, RSL completes its maiden sale of software to a retail store and receives a price of ₹ 12,000.
- On March 21, RSL pays ₹ 2,000 to its creditors for supplies.
- On March 29, RSL pays salaries to its employees, amounting to ₹ 4,000 and as office rent ₹ 1,000.
- On March 30, RSL delivers a software package for a shoe shop. The customer agrees to pay the price of ₹ 8,000 a week later.
- On March 31, Ram withdraws ₹ 3,000 for his personal use. At the end of the month you are required to prepare its income statement.

2nd Period[17]:

- In 2nd period RSL made a Credit Sales of ₹ 10,000 and Cash Sales of ₹ 5,000
- Whereas, salaries, rent remain the same and paid as in the 1st period.

Adjustments for the 1st period –

- On the last day Closing Stock was ₹ 5,000
- Depreciation ₹ 2,000
- Interest Charge was 5% per month

Adjustments for the 2nd period –

- On the last day Closing Stock was ₹ 4,000
- Depreciation remained ₹ 2,000
- Interest Charge was 5% per month
- The Interest paid was ₹ 2,000 and Loan was repaid with ₹ 2,000

Solution: 1st Period

The first transaction wherein, Ram & others invest ₹ 50,000 in cash in RSL would not influence the income statement.

The second transaction involves, RSL taking a loan of ₹ 20,000 from Venugopal. Since, an income statement is prepared to record the changes to an organizations owners' equity (due to its business operations) there would be no effect on the income statement.

Similarly, the transactions involving RSL purchasing two computers and also some supplies would also not change the income statement.

The next transaction on March 19, wherein RSL completes its maiden sale of software to a retail store and receives a price of ₹ 12,000 would result in the income statement having a sale of a similar amount.

RSL pays ₹ 2,000 to its creditors for supplies. This transaction would lead to a change in the cash position of the company but would not lead to a change its income statement.

On March 29, RSL pays salaries to its employees, amounting to ₹ 4,000 and as office rent ₹ 1,000. Assuming these payments are for the whole month, would result in the expense side of the income statement consisting of these two items.

[17] Transaction solution and adjustments for period 1 has been illustrated via equation method. Table 10.8 and the income statement in standard format in Table 10.9 has been given for the reader's better understanding.

RSL delivers a software package for a shoe shop worth ₹ 8,000 and the customer agrees to pay the price a week later. The result of this transaction would be an increase in the revenue of the company by a similar amount.

On March 31, the owner withdraws ₹ 3,000 from the profits of the company. We consider the same to be dividend. A result of all the above transactions would be the following:

Table 10.1 ***Ram Software Limited***

Profit & Loss Account for the Period 1st to 31st March (all figures in ₹)

Rent Expense	1,000	Sales Net	20,000
Salaries Expense	4,000		
Operating Profit	15,000		
Interest Expense	0	Operating Profit	15,000
Net Profit	15,000		
Withdrawals (OR Dividends)	3,000	Net Profit	15,000
Retained Earnings to Balance Sheet	12,000		

Matching principle states that we need to adjust the above figures for the depreciation in the fixed assets (having made use of them for 25 days). Also, we need to take stock of the remaining stationary and other supplies for necessary adjustments.

For example, if we were to decide on depreciation of the computers by ₹ 1,700 (assume) and also found that supplies worth ₹ 2,300 to be consumed by RSL, this would have resulted in the income statement being restated as follows.

Above we have shown the income statement for the 1st period. In the last page, readers will find the comparison between the balance sheet and the income statement for the 2nd period in the equation method.

Table 10.2 ***Ram Software Limited***

Profit & Loss Account for the Period 1st to 31st March (all figures in ₹)

Rent Expense	1,000	Sales Net	20,000
Salaries Expense	4,000		
Depreciation Expense	1,700		
Supplies Consumed	2,300		
Operating Profit	11,000		
Interest Expense	0	Operating Profit	11,000
Net Profit	11,000		
Withdrawals (OR Dividends)	3,000	Net Profit	11,000
Retained Earnings to Balance Sheet	8,000		

Example 2: Mitu & Tikan Textiles

From the following information provided for the year ending by Mitu & Tikan Textiles, prepare a profit and loss account for the financial year 2009:

Particulars	Amount (₹)	Particulars	Amount (₹)
Capital Employed	200,000	Opening Stock	60,000
Machinery Purchased	100,000	Furniture	50,000
Cash Purchases for the Year	175,000	Cash Sales	305,000
Payable to suppliers of material	25,000	Adv. Expenses	5,000
Credit Sales for the Year	15,000	Discount allowed	5,000
Cash Discount on purchases	15,000	Closing Stock	15,000
Salary Paid	25,000	Receivable from customers	15,000
Credit Purchases for the year	25,000		

Solution

This is a problem which will be solved by identifying the individual items and allocating them to the appropriate side of either the balance sheet or income summary in the following manner:

- Capital employed is not considered in the preparation of the profit and loss account, as we have seen in the previous chapter that it is a balance sheet item. Similar is the case of machinery purchased and furniture (both would be part of assets).
- As explained in this chapter, purchases include all purchases, whether on cash or on credit. The amount payable to the supplier of raw materials is shown in the balance sheet as sundry creditors (or trade payables). Hence, purchases for the year amount to ₹ 200,000 (cash purchases ₹ 175,000 *plus* credit purchases ₹ 25,000).
- Similarly, sales include the total amount of sales for cash as well as credit. The amount receivable from customers is shown in the balance sheet as sundry debtors, as a part of the current assets. Thus, the sales for the year are ₹ 320,000 (cash sales ₹ 305,000 and credit sales ₹ 15,000).
- Discount allowed is an expense for the business, and so it is charged against the revenue for the period[18].

[18]Alternatively, it can be shown as a reduction from the sales. In that case, net sales amount would be ₹ 315,000 (i.e., 320,000 – 5,000).

- Similarly, discount received is a benefit enjoyed by the business and it can be treated as revenue for the period[19].

Now, we are in a position to prepare the profit and loss account for Mitu & Tikan Textiles (Table 10.3).

Table 10.3 ***Profit and Loss Account of Mitu & Tikan Textiles for the Year Ending 31st December 2012***

Particulars	Amount (₹)	Particulars	Amount (₹)
To opening stock	60,000	By sales during the year	320,000
To purchases for the year	200,000	By discount received	15,000
To discount allowed	5,000	By closing stock	15,000
To salary	25,000		
To advertisement expenses	5,000		
To profit for the year	55,000		
Total	**350,000**	**Total**	**350,000**

Example 3: Bombay Club

Table 10.4 shows the receipts and payments account of Bombay Club for the year ended March 31, 2012.

Table 10.4 ***Receipts and Payments Account of Bombay Club for theYear Ended March 31, 2012***

Receipts **Payments**

Particulars	Amount (₹)	Particulars	Amount (₹)
Opening bank balance	15,000	Furniture purchased	20,000
Loan from Malcolm D'Souza	10,000	Insurance premium paid	5,000
Membership fee received*	55,000	Salary paid	19,500
Entrance fee received	18,000	Rent paid	12,000
Proceeds from sale of investments	125,000	Electricity paid	2,000
		Printing and stationery	1,850
		Sundry expenses	3,000
		Closing bank balance	159,650
Total	**223,000**	**Total**	**223,000**

***Membership fees of ₹ 55,000 consisted of the following:**

Previous dues of membership fees:	₹ 5,000
Membership fees for the year:	₹ 40,000
Advance membership for the next year:	₹ 10,000

[19]Alternatively, it can be shown as a reduction from the total purchases for the period, making the amount of net purchases to be ₹ 185,000 (i.e., ₹ 200,000 – ₹ 15,000). Readers can calculate and verify that in both the alternative treatments, net profit of the business will remain the same.

The additional information provided to you is

	31-03-2011	31-03-2012
Rent outstanding	₹ 1,200	₹ 2,400
Membership fees (not received)	₹ 5,000	—

- Cost of investments sold ₹ 20,000. These investments were purchased long back (before FY2011).
- Loan was taken from Malcolm on June 30, 2011, on interest of 10percent per annum.
- Value of furniture on March 31, 2011, was ₹ 16,000. It is noted that new furniture was purchased on June 30, 2011. Depreciation on furniture is to be provided at 20 percent per annum.
- The accounting policy of the club provides that 30 percent of the entrance fee is to be treated as revenue and the balance be capitalized.
- The capital and other funds balance as on March 31, 2011 is ₹ 54,800.

You are required to prepare a balance sheet as on March 31,2011, income and expenditure account for the period ended March 31, 2012,and a balance sheet as on that date.

Solution

This is a complicated problem but it reflects situations usually faced by finance executives. It can be solved in various ways. We illustrate one way of cracking the problem. It involves preparing the balance sheet of Bombay Club for FY2011 and then working on the financial statements of FY2012 by deciphering information given in the problem.

In the previous chapter, we have seen the way in which a balance sheet is prepared. We use the same method here. Based on the information provided we can say that the amount of fee due but not received at the end of the year is a current asset (receivable). Similarly, the bank balance, furniture, and investments would be part of the assets side of the balance sheet. Regarding other items, we know that the amount of rent payable is a current liability, so it is included under the head liabilities. In addition, capital and other funds would also be part of the liabilities side of the balance sheet. The opening balance sheet is, thus, presented in Table 10.5.

Now, let us consider the following revenue items which effect the income and expenditure statement of the current year:

Table 10.5 **Bombay Club Balance Sheet as on 31st March 2011**

Assets	Amount (₹)	Liabilities	Amount (₹)
Current assets Bank balance Membership fee receivable *Non-current assets* Investments Furniture	 15,000 5,000 20,000 16,000	Current liabilities Outstanding rent *Owner's equity and funds* Capital and other funds	 1,200 54,800
Total assets	**56,000**	**Total liabilities and owner's equity**	**56,000**

- Total rent paid during FY 2012 is ₹ 12,000. We know that out of this, an amount equal to 1,200 relates to the previous year, as the same amount was outstanding as on March 31, 2011. Further, the amount of rent outstanding as on March 31, 2012—₹ 2,400—is the rent payable and hence, pertains to the current period. Therefore, the actual rent for the year 2012 is ₹ 13,200 [₹ 12,000 + (2,400 – 1,200)].

Or

Rent paid	= ₹ 12,000
Add: Current year outstanding	= ₹ 2,400
Less: Last year outstanding	= ₹ 1,200
Actual Rent	= ₹ 13,200

- The accounting policy of the club states that 30 percent of the entrance fee is to be treated as revenue and the balance is capitalized. As a result, 30 percent of ₹ 18,000 (or ₹ 5,400) is to be considered as revenue and the balance 70 percent (or ₹ 12,600) is to be capitalized and added in capital and other funds.
- Depreciation on furniture is calculated as follows:
  On opening balance (for 12 months) 16,000 × 20% = ₹ 3,200
  On purchases during the year (nine months)
  20,000 × 20% × 9/12 = ₹ 3,000
  Total ₹ 6,200
- Interest on loan is calculated for a period of nine months at10percent per annum. Since the amount is related to the current period, it is treated as an expense and as the amount is yet to be paid; it is also taken to the balance sheet as a current liability.

Now, the income and expenditure account of Bombay Club for the year ended March 31, 2011, is presented in Table 10.6.

Table 10.6 *Bombay Club Income and Expenditure Account for the Period March 31, 2012*

Particulars	Amount (₹)	Particulars	Amount (₹)
To salary	19,500	By entrance fee (30% revenue)	5,400
To rent	13,200		
To electricity	2,000	By profit on sale of investment	105,000
To printing and stationery	1,850		
To sundry expenses	3,000	By membership fee	40,000
To insurance paid	5,000		
To depreciation	6,200		
To interest payable	750		
Excess of income over expenditure*	98,900		
Total	**150,400**	**Total**	**150,400**

- The excess of income over expenditure is the balancing figure. It is similar to net profit.

After preparing the income and expenditure account, we can prepare the balance sheet without any difficulty, in Table 10.7.

Table 10.7 *Bombay Club Balance Sheet as on March 31, 2012 (All figures in ₹)*

Assets	Amount (₹)	Liabilities	Amount (₹)
Current assets		***Current liabilities***	
Bank balance	159,650	Rent payable	
Non-current assets		Interest payable (on loan)	2,400
Furniture Opening balance ₹ 16,000 Add: Purchases ₹ 20,000 Total gross furniture ₹ 36,000 Less: Accumulated depreciation ₹ 6,200	29,800	Advance membership fees	750
		Long-term liabilities	
		Loan	10,000
		Owners' equity and funds	
		Capital and other funds	10,000
		Opening balance ₹ 54,800 Add: Entrance fee ₹ 12,600	67,400
		Surplus	98,900
Total assets	**189,450**	**Total liabilities & Owner's equity**	**189,450**

It would be a good idea to re-read Table 10.8 and mull over the various solutions.

Table 10.8 ***Ram Software Limited: Accounting Equation of Balance Sheet and Profit & Loss Statement for each transaction of Period 1 and 2***

Ram Software Limited:														
	Assets					**Liabilities**			**Owners' Equity**					
Date	Cash	Receivables	Supplies	Computer	=	Trade Payables	Interest Payable	Loan, Venu	Contributed Capital	Reserves, Past	Profit for the Period	Rev.	Exp.	Dividends
Ram Software Limited: Accounting Equation for each transaction of Period 1														
1-Mar	50,000				=				50,000					
2-Mar	20,000				=			20,000						
3-Mar	(58,000)			58,000	=									
4-Mar			6,000		=	6,000								
19-Mar	12,000				=							12,000		
21-Mar	(2,000)				=	(2,000)								
29-Mar	(5,000)				=								5,000	
30-Mar		8,000			=							8,000		
31-Mar	(3,000)				=									3,000
Unadjusted Trial Balance	14,000	8,000	6,000	58,000	=	4,000	0	20,000	50,000	0	12,000	20,000	5,000	3,000

(Contd.)

Table 10.8 **(Contd.)**

Ram Software Limited:														
	Assets					**Liabilities**			**Owners' Equity**					
Adjustments for Period 1 of Ram **Software Limited**					=									
Supplies, closing stock adjustment			(1,000)		=								1,000	
Depreciation, computers				(2,000)	=								2,000	
Accured Interest					=		1,000						1,000	
Adjusted Trial Balance	14,000	8,000	5,000	56,000	=	4,000	1,000	20,000	50,000	0	8,000	20,000	9,000	3,000
Profit & Loss Statement for Period 1					=						**Profit for the Period**	**Rev.**	**Exp.**	**Dividends**
					=						**8,000**	**20,000**	**9,000**	**3,000**
Balance Sheet at the end of Period 1					=									
	Assets				=	**Liabilities**			**Owners' Equity**					
	Cash	**Receivables**	**Supplies**	**Computer**	=	**Trade Payables**	**Interest Payable**	**Loan, Venu**	**Contributed Capital**	**Reserves**				

(*Contd.*)

Table 10.8 ***(Contd.)***

Ram Software Limited:														
	Assets					**Liabilities**			**Owners' Equity**					
	14,000	**8,000**	**5,000**	**56,000**	**=**	**4,000**	**1,000**	**20,000**	**50,000**	**8,000**				
Ram Software Limited: Accounting Equation for each transaction of Period 2														
	Cash	Receivables	Supplies	Computer	=	Trade Payables	Interest Payable	Loan, Venu	Contributed Capital	Reserves, Past	Profit for the Period	Rev.	Exp.	Dividends
Opening Balances	14,000	8,000	5,000	56,000	=	4,000	1,000	20,000	50,000	8,000				
Credit Sales		10,000			=							10,000		
Cash Sales	5,000				=							5,000		
Salaries Expense	(4,000)				=								4,000	
Rent Expense	(1,200)				=								1,000	
Interest Paid	(2,000)				=		(2,000)							
Loan Repaid	(2,000)				=			(2,000)						
Adjustment, **Depreciation for** Period 2				(2,000)	=								2,000	

(*Contd.*)

Table 10.8 ***(Contd.)***

Ram Software Limited:														
	Assets					Liabilities			Owners' Equity					
Adjustment, Accrued Interest for Period 2					=		1,000						1,000	
Supplies, closing stock adjustment for Period 2			(1,000)		=								1,000	
Adjusted Trial Balance	9,800	18,000	4,000	54,000	=	4,000	0	18,000	50,000	8,000	6,000	15,000	9,000	0
Profit & Loss Statement for Period 2					=						**Profit for the Period**	**Rev.**	**Exp.**	**Dividends**
					=						**6,000**	**15,000**	**9,000**	**0**
Balance Sheet at the end of Period 2					=									
	Assets				=	**Liabilities**			**Owners' Equity**					
	Cash	**Receivables**	**Supplies**	**Computer**	=	**Trade Payables**	**Interest Payable**	**Loan, Venu**	**Contributed Capital**	**Reserves**				
	9,800	**18,000**	**4,000**	**54,000**	**=**	**4,000**	**0**	**18,000**	**50,000**	**14,000**				

Given above is the equation method of the Balance sheet and Profit and Loss statement of the financial transactions of Ram Software for two periods--for comparing the financial progress of the company. Since, while making a profit and loss statement, the balance sheet items need to judged, similarly an accountant would do the vice-versa while making an income statement too.

Below is the Profit and Loss statement of Ram Software for the two periods shown through standard format in Table 10.9. Readers should hereon be able to compare the income statement shown in Table 10.8 with the one shown in Table 10.9.

Table 10.9 ***Ram Software Limited:Standard Format***

Profit & Loss Statement for the Periods 1 and 2

	Period 1	**Period 2**
Item	Amount	Amount
Sales	**20,000**	**15,000**
Less: Cost of Goods Sold (including Salaries)	4,000	4,000
Gross Profit	16,000	11,000
Less: Sales Expenses	0	0
Less: Administration Expenses (includes Rent Expenses)	1,000	1,000
Less: General Expenses (includes Supplies Consumed)	1,000	1,000
EBIDTA	14,000	9,000
Less: Depreciation & Amortization Expenses	2,000	2,000
Operating Profit	12,000	7,000
Add: Other Income	0	0
Adjusted for Extraordinary & Past Period Items	0	0
EBIT	12,000	7,000
Less: Interest Expenses	1,000	1,000
Profit Before Tax (PBT)	11,000	6,000
Less: Income Tax Expenses	0	0
Profit After Tax (PAT ... a.k.a. Net Income)	**11,000**	**6,000**
Less: Dividends for the Period	3,000	0
Profit/Loss Transferred to the Balance Sheet	**8,000**	**6,000**

Summary and Exercises

Summary

In this book, we developed and examined the income statement. Studying a company's income statement can help managers, investors, creditors, and analysts to form an understanding of the business's performance and profitability. This statement shows net profit or earnings generated by a company during an accounting period. To sum up, it measures the management's contribution during an accounting period by showing the income generated from the assets.

The profit and loss account summarizes the revenues and expenses of an accounting period. As a result of this summary, it shows net profit or net loss earned or suffered by a company during the period. The reader of this account gets an idea of the cost structure and profitability during the accounting period.

However, the income statement has come under some criticism in recent years because of the two main figures—income and expenses which are often obscured by accounting adjustments and subjective estimates by many analysts. Usage of expanded reporting standards limits companies' ability to overstate revenue or understate expenses. In any case, rather than relying on the income statement alone, users should examine all three major financial statements to gain further information about a company's results.

Exercises

The net profit, after payment of dividends, shows the amount retained and hence, links the balance sheet with the profit and loss account.

1. Answer the following by filling in the blanks.
   1.1 The profit and loss account is a summary of/for an accounting period.

1.2 Realization in accounting is the basis of recognition.

1.3 Income measurement is achieved by matching to __________.

1.4 Costs relating to realized revenues are considered as _________.

1.5 Recognized revenue the owner(s)' equity.

1.6 Expenses result in of the owner(s)' equity.

1.7 Expenses could be recognized in relation to realized or a _________ _______of accounting period.

1.8 Resources received for sale of goods or services are referred to as _____________.

1.9 Resources used up in producing goods or services are called ____________.

1.10 Wages are an example of __________.

2. Multiple Choice Questions.

2.1 Goods Purchased – ₹ 10,000, Sales ₹ 9,000 Margin 20% on cost. Closing Stock - ?

(a) (1,000) (b) 1,000
(c) 2,500 (d) 2,800

2.2 If the opening inventory is understated and the closing inventory is overstated, the profit would:

(a) Increase (b) Decrease
(c) No Change (d) None

2.3 Inventories consist of:

(a) Raw Materials (b) Work-in-Progress
(c) Finished Goods (d) All of the above

2.4 On which principle will the determination of expenses for the accounting period depend?

(a) Periodicity (b) Matching
(c) Realization (d) Accrual

2.5 Revenue from sale of a product is generally realized when:

(a) Sale is made (b) It is Manufactured
(c) Cash is collected (d) It is Delivered

2.6 The depletion method of depreciation is adopted on:

(a) Land & Building (b) Computers
(c) Goodwill (d) Mines & Quarries

2.7 Which among the followings is assumed to be non-depreciating?

(a) Land (b) Goodwill
(c) Cash (d) Plant & Machinery

2.8 Owners' Equity would change as a result of:
 (a) Decrease of Creditors
 (b) Payment of salaries & wages
 (c) Increase of Debtors
 (d) Purchase of Fixed Assets

3. Relate items in Column A to all items in Column B.

Table 1 ***Match the Following***

A	B
a. Depreciation expense b. Gross sales c. Sales returns/allowances d. Prepaid expense e. Discounts f. Give effect on return of goods by customers. g. Dividends	1) An appropriation of profits. 2) Unexpired cost of the period 3) Invoice notation, "2/15, n/30" 4) Adjustments to recorded sales. 5) Invoice value goods sold during the period. 6) Reduction from invoice price. 7) Expiration of cost of fixed assets.

4. Classify each item listed in column A into one of the following categories – (a) Operating revenue (b) Non-operating revenue (c) Cost of goods sold (d) Selling and distribution expense (e) General administrative expense (f) Appropriation of profit and (g) Not related to profit and loss account, by appropriately marking them in column B. Assume that the information relates to a small manufacturing firm.

Table 2 ***Classification of Items***

A	B
Raw material consumed	
Interest received	
Dividends received	
Wages paid to manufacturing workers	
Carriage on goods sold	
Carriage on goods purchased	
Salary of clerical staff	
Rent for office	
Power and fuel	
Selling agents commission	
Advertising	

(Contd.)

Table 2 **(Contd.)**

A	B
Auditor(s) fees	
Sales tax	
Municipal rates on office premises	
Profit on sale of fixed assets	
Power used in administrative office	
Sales discount	
Purchase returns and allowances	
Dividends paid	
Interest expense on loans	

5. Shyam's Enterprise
Table 3 shows the summarized profit and loss account of Shyam's Enterprise for five consecutive periods. Complete the same by supplying the missing information.

Table 3 ***Summarized Profit and Loss Account Of Shyam's Enterprise (Figures in ₹ '000's)***

Year →	1	2	3	4	5
Sales	1,000	?	3,000	?	5,000
Cost of goods sold	500	800	?	2,500	3,000
Gross profit	?	700	1,000	1,500	?
Administrative expenses	100	?	400	400	?
Selling and distribution	150	200	?	500	600
Operating profit	?	200	400	?	1,000
Other income	150	?	200	?	500
Net profit before tax	?	300	?	1,000	?
Provision for corporate tax	200	?	300	?	750
Profit aftertax	?	200	?	500	?
Dividend	50	?	10	?	?
Surplus to retained earnings (i.e., balance sheet)	?	100	?	50	500

6. Shantanu Real Estate Brokers
The summary of financial data for each transaction of Shantanu Real Estate Brokers is presented in Table 4 in the extended balance sheet equation form. Describe the possible transactions for each entry.

Table 4 **Transactions of Shantanu Real Estate Brokers (all figures in ₹ '000's)**

	Cash +	Accounts receivable +	Office furniture	= Accounts payable	+ Shantanu, capital
(i)	100				100
(ii)			200		200
(iii)	–50		+ 250	200	
(iv)	+ 600				+ 600
(v)	–100			–100	
(vi)	–200				–200
(vii)		+200			+200
(viii)	+100	+ 100			+200
(ix)	+150	-150			
(x)	–200				–200
(xi)	–100			–100	

7. Profit and loss account of Hindustan Unilever Limited

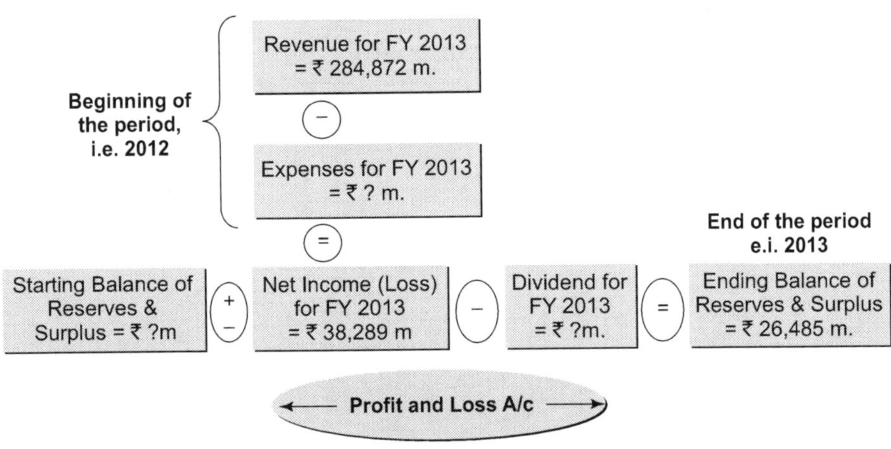

Figure 1 ***Hindustan Unilever Limited Income Statement FY2012-2013 and its relation with Balance Sheet FY2012-2013 (all figures in million)***

Above is the income statement of Hindustan Unilever Limited and its relation with the balance sheet of the same for FY2012-2013. Chapter 5, Fig. 5.2 shows the income statement and its relation with the balance sheet of the firm for FY 2011-12. Hence, calculate and fill in the blanks with the correct amounts following up with the previous accounting year's data.

8. Trends in income statement of Reliance Industries Limited
In Chapter 4, page 46, we introduced you to the income statement of *Reliance Industries Limited, based* on the income statements provided therein (from FY2011 to FY2013), please mark whether the following statements in Table 6 are true or false by marking 'T' or 'F' opposite each statement.

Table 5 ***Performance of Reliance Industries Limited***

8.1	While sales of Reliance Industries Limited increased in both years (FY2012 and FY2013, on a year-on-year basis), the company's net profit did not show the same trend.	(T/F)
8.2	Looking at all the components of Reliance Industries Limited's income statement, we can say that 'other income' of reliance industries limited had the biggest jump from FY2011 to FY2013 (in percentage terms).	(T/F)
8.3	If gross profit margin is defined as gross profit divided by net sales/Revenue from operations then one could say that Reliance Industries Limited had a gross margin of above 20 percent for all the three years	(T/F)
8.4	The company's depreciation Amortization expenses have been consistently decreasing (in percentage terms).	(T/F)
8.5	The company's deferred tax has been consistently increasing (in percentage terms).	(T/F)
8.6	The net profit margin of the company (defined as net profit divided by gross revenue) has been consistently decreasing	(T/F)
8.7	The company's operating profit margin (defined as operating income by net sale/ Revenue from operations) has been consistently decreasing.	(T/F)

9. Common-Size Figures

Table 6 ***Common-Size Figures of the Income Statement of four major retail companies of India.***

	Raymond Limited		**Reliance Industries Ltd.**		**Infosys Limited**	
Financial Year ⇒	**2013**	**2012**	**2013**	**2012**	**2013**	**2012**
Sales / Income From Operations	**100.0%**	**100.0%**	**100.0%**	**100.0%**	**100.0%**	**100.0%**
Less: Cost of Goods Sold	57.7%	54.2%	83.7%	83.2%	65.2%	61.9%
Gross Profit	42.3%	45.8%	16.3%	16.8%	34.8%	38.1%

(Contd.)

Table 6 **(Contd.)**

	Raymond Limited		Reliance Industries Ltd.		Infosys Limited	
Financial Year ⇒	**2013**	**2012**	**2013**	**2012**	**2013**	**2012**
Less: Sales, General & Administration Expenses	32.8%	32.8%	8.0%	7.1%	6.0%	6.3%
EBIDTA (Earnings Before Interest, Depreciation, Taxes & Amortization)	**9.5%**	**13.0%**	**8.3%**	**9.7%**	**28.8%**	**31.8%**
Less: Depreciation & Amortization Expenses	4.6%	4.5%	2.8%	3.5%	2.7%	2.8%
Operating Profit	4.9%	8.5%	5.5%	6.3%	26.1%	29.0%
Adjusted for Other Income & Similar Items	1.8%	2.0%	2.0%	1.7%	5.9%	5.6%
Adjusted for Exceptional Items	-0.7%	0.0%	0.0%	-0.1%	-0.2%	0.0%
EBIT (Earnings Before Interest Tax)	6.0%	10.4%	7.5%	7.9%	31.7%	34.7%
Less: Interest Expenses & Financial Charges	4.7%	4.5%	0.9%	0.8%	0.0%	0.0%
EBT (Earnings Before Tax, also known as, Profit Before Tax i.e., PBT)	**0**	**0**	**0**	**0**	**0**	**0**
Less: Corporate Income Tax Expenses	0.6%	1.7%	1.3%	1.6%	8.4%	10.0%
Net Profit (also, Profit After Tax i.e., PAT)	**0.7%**	**4.3%**	**5.3%**	**5.5%**	**23.4%**	**24.7%**

(Contd.)

Questions

1. Which company is facing fewer losses compared to the other companies and why?
2. Which company has the highest profit margin among the four?
3. Which company has spent the highest while selling their products, such as on advertisement, packing, etc.?

4. Which company among the three will strive to earn profit over loss?

5. Why does Infosys pay more corporate tax (Refer Chapter 7, Table 7.3)?

Keys

1. Fill in the blanks:
   1.1 Revenues, Expense
   1.2 Revenue
   1.3 Expenses, Realized Revenues of the Period
   1.4 Expenses
   1.5 Increases
   1.6 Decreases
   1.7 Revenues, Cost Expiration
   1.8 Revenue
   1.9 Assets
   1.10 Expense

2. MCQ Keys:
   2.1 (c)
   2.2 (a)
   2.3 (d)
   2.4 (b)
   2.5 (a)
   2.6 (d)
   2.7 (a) & (c)
   2.8 (b)

3. Match the following (we pick the best fit):

Column A	->	Column B
A	->	7
B	->	5
C	->	3
D	->	2
E	->	6
F	->	4
G	->	1

4. Classify the items:

Column A	Column B
Raw material consumed	C
Interest received	B
Dividends received	B
Wages paid to manufacturing workers	C
Carriage on goods sold	D
Carriage on goods purchased	B
Salary of clerical staff	E
Rent for office	E
Power and fuel	C
Selling agent's commission	D
Advertising	D
Auditors' fees	E
Sales tax	A
Municipal rates on office premises	E
Profit on sale of fixed assets	B
Power used in administrative office	E
Sales discount	G
Purchase returns and allowances	C
Dividends paid	F
Interest expense on loans	Financial expenses

5. Shyam's Enterprise

Year →	1	2	3	4	5
Sales		1,500		4,000	
Cost of goods sold			2,000		
Gross Profit	500				2,000
Administrative expenses		400			400
Selling and distribution			300		
Operating Profit	250			600	
Other Income		100		400	
Net Profit before tax	400		600		1,500
Provision for Corporate tax		100		500	
Profit aftertax	200		300		750
Dividend		100		450	250
Retained earnings	200	400	700	1200	1,950

6. Shantanu Real Estate Brokers Possible transactions:

i. Shantanu contributed ₹ 100,000 as capital to his business. So, the cash position has increased.

ii. Fixed asset to this business has been shown as ₹ 200,000.

iii. Office furniture worth ₹ 250,000 has been purchased, but only ₹ 50,000 has been paid through cash. The remaining amount, i.e., ₹ 200,000 is on credit.

iv. Shantanu again contributed ₹ 600,000 as capital.

v. An amount of ₹ 100,000 was paid to the creditors. So, the cash position has decreased.

vi. Shantanu withdraws ₹ 200,000 from the capital account. So, the cash position has been decreased by an equivalent amount.

vii. The firm purchased something worth ₹ 200,000 on credit

viii. Shantanu again contributed ₹ 200,000 as capital, but only ₹ 100,000 in cash and rest on agreement for taking service worth ₹ 100,000 from the firm.

ix. ₹ 150,000 worth accounts receivables were realized. Hence, the cash position increased.

x. Shantanu withdraws ₹ 200,000 from capital account.

xi. ₹ 100,000 worth accounts payable were settled. Hence, the cash position decreased.

7. Profit and loss account of Hindustan Unilever Limited

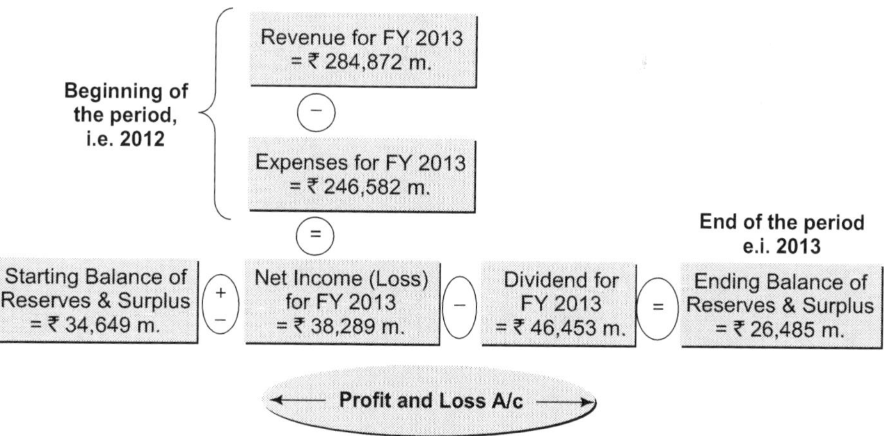

Hindustan Unilever Limited Income Statement FY2012-2013 and its relation with Balance Sheet FY2012-2013 (all figures in million)

8. Trends in income statement of Reliance Industries Limited

8.1 False

Sales in 2013 were 10.8% more as compared to 34.9% in 2012, whereas there was an increase in profit in 2013 as compared to profit in 2012.

8.2 False

Other income fell by 27.07% in 2013 from 143.6% in 2012.

8.3 False

The gross profit margin was 18.3% in 2013, 18.5% in 2012 and 24% in 2011. It ranged between 18% to 24%.

8.4 True

It declined by 12% in 2012 and it further declined to 9.4% in 2013%.

8.5 False

It rose by 25.34% in 2012 but declined in 2013 by 99%.

8.6 True

Net profit margin was 7.1% in 2011 and declined to 5.4% in 2012. It further declined to 5% in 2013.

8.7 True

Operating profit margin was 9% in 2011 and declined to 7% in 2012. It further declined to 6.6% in 2013.

9. Common-Size Figures

1. Infosys Limited is facing fewer losses due to its operating profit being the highest among the three companies in comparison to the depreciation and other such expenses.
2. Infosys Limited has the highest profit margin since its net profit is the highest, which indicates a higher net profit margin. (Refer Chapter 7, Table 7.3)
3. Reliance Industries Limited has spent the most on the surrounding factors for selling its products. Due to this, the company projects its COGS as 83.7% in 2013.
4. Infosys Limited will win the race of earning profit over loss in the long run since the company has been more or less constant in its performance.
5. The corporate income tax is computed at a pre-decided corporate tax rate announced by the finance minister (in his/her budget speech—say, 33%-34%) – based on a company's profit before tax. Since Infosys has better PBT compared with other companies.

Index

Authors' Profiles

Dr. N. Ramachandran is the Director of Kochi Business School, Kochi, Kerala. An MBA and Ph.D. from and a fellow of IIM Calcutta. Dr. Ramachandran has over three decades of academic experience at his alma mater and Asian Institute of Technology (AIT), Bangkok, where he was also the Chief Internal Auditor. He has been a consultant to government and non-government agencies in various countries, including India, Thailand, Laos, Sri Lanka, Cambodia and Vietnam. His area of interest includes Financial Structure of Industries, Corporate Financial Accounting and Strategic Cost Management.

Dr. Ram Kumar Kakani is a Professor at the Lal Bahadur Shastri National Academy of Administration, with a past corporate experience. A fellow of IIM Calcutta, Dr. Kakani has been a resident academician at international institutions in Copenhagen, Dubai, Lagos and Singapore and has conducted research with the support of Aditya Birla Research Centre (ABRC) of the London Business School and National Stock Exchange of India. A recipient of the AIMS Best Young Teacher Award (2005) and ranked among the top 1% of the Social Science Research Network (SSRN) authors. His area of interest includes Accounting Analysis, Corporate Finance, Corporate Strategy, and Study of Business Groups.

25815578R00069

Made in the USA
San Bernardino, CA
11 November 2015